CALLED BY THE FIRE

I couldn't be more proud of Josh and his wife Olivia. They're the real deal. From the moment we met they've proved passionate, sincere, and fearless in their calling, which is one very dear to our family: to bring Jesus to the lost and the hurting in places where his name may never have been heard. As they have chosen to go where the need for heaven's reality is so clear, so in simple faith they have seen that reality break forth time and time again. Wherever you may be called, their testimony will edify you.

HEIDI G. BAKER, PH.D.
Co-founder and Executive Chairman of the Board, Iris Global
Author: *Compelled by Love, Birthing the Miraculous* and *Always Enough*

I have met so many Christians who believe that the miracles of Jesus ceased when He went to the Father. They need to read Josh Muse's book, *Called by the Fire*. It is literally teeming with miracles: demonstrating over and over the supernatural multiplying of food for those literally dying of hunger, healings from every imaginable disease, the dead brought back to life, deliverance from satan's web of demons for those who had been trapped and unable to function for years, restoration for untold numbers who had been unable to walk or talk all of their lives.

His book showed so beautifully the truth: There is no fire without sacrifice; no glory without the process; and no mantle without the mandate. Too often modern Christians are enjoying Jesus as their Savior and their friend, but Josh's book brings out so clearly that when Jesus came we now have access to the all-powerful King and miracle worker.

If your walk with God is stale, lifeless and unexciting, it will only take a few pages of *Called by the Fire* to infuse the joy and excitement that Christianity was meant to bring.

PEGGY JOYCE RUTH
Co-founder of Better Living Ministries
Author: *Psalm 91; God's Umbrella of Protection*

Josh Muse is a man on fire and it's contagious! I love this book. Not only will it cause a deep hunger within you for the same glorious fire of the Holy Spirit in your life, but it will cause a desire for unwavering obedience to the call of Jesus into a supernatural life of extraordinary adventure with Him. Josh's powerful stories, full of real-life testimonies of God's miracles, together with his amazing understanding of the scriptures, fuel a burning desire within, to shine ever more brightly with Jesus' glory and for His glory. Reading this book will set you on fire to set your world on fire.

DUNCAN SMITH
President Catch The Fire World
Author: *Consumed with Holy Fire*

God speaks to Zerubbabel in Zechariah 4:6 «Not by might, nor by power, but by my Spirit, says the Lord of hosts». As I have traveled the world for the last 22 years, I have witnessed a common theme amongst those who God is using. *Called by the Fire* is not only an encouragement to live a Spirit-directed life, but a reminder of the simplicity of being directed by God. Josh Muse shares firsthand of what an obedient life dedicated to Jesus looks like and the fruit that is produced. Grab a cup of coffee and your favorite highlighter and get ready for God to call you deeper.

WILL HART
Chief Operations Officer Iris Global
Author: *God Runner*

I've known Josh and Olivia Muse to be a new breed of apostolic missionaries that God is raising up in our generation. Their commitment and lifestyle are a model for us all and will be an inspiration to release thousands into the regions beyond. This book is filled with adventure, vulnerability, sincerity and acts of faith. The stories have challenged me personally and I know this narrative will be a challenge to courage for all of us in the body of Christ during this season that the world is going through.

Thank you, Josh and Olivia, for living out your faith to your generation.

DAN SLADE
Global Missions Ambassador Catch The Fire World

Called by the Fire was not written by a man in a swivel chair surrounded by books, but by a man on fire riding a chariot on fire. Joshua tells us about his experiences and about the experiences of the men in the Bible like Moses or Peter, and it is hard to see where one story starts and the other ends because Jesus is still raising the dead, setting free the demonized chained to posts, healing the blind and the deaf, and multiplying food. Joshua writes about his wounds and scars, too, which cleanses the pages from hype and fills the story with a humility that tells us, "You can live this wonderful life, too." I wish I had this book when I was starting in the mission field, but we have it now! I have not heard such a clear call to the mission field in America since the days of Keith Green.

You must understand that this book is an invitation to live in the fire of God. You can refuse, which may harden your heart, or you can say yes and get ready for a chariot ride.

ANDREW MCMILLAN
Comunidad Cristiana de Fe
Medellín, Colombia.

As a pastor and church planter for over 30 years and leader in international networks with extensive ministry experience around the world, I've gotten to know many revivalists and ministers. I can sincerely say I've never met anyone like Josh Muse. I've worked extensively with him and the Kaleo ministry team over the past few years and have found them to be the most fruitful I've ever seen. In regards to salvations, transformed lives, church multiplication, and missions work, they consistently impress me. Knowing them personally, I have also seen their integrity and dedication in many ways. Some of the stories in this book may sound unbelievable, but let me assure you they are real. I have seen first-hand some of the miracles that have occurred with the Kaleo team and these are the most legit, on fire, dedicated, and passionate ministers I've ever worked with. I encourage you to read this book with an open mind and a hungry heart. The world and the Church desperately need every Christ follower to be as passionate in the pursuit of the fire of God's awesome presence as demonstrated in these stories. Let the words of this book and the Spirit of God encourage us to live in such a way as to have equally compelling testimonies of God's miraculous provision!

CAMERON WRIGHT
Pastor New Day Community Church &
Director of Harvest Alliance North America

Josh has been an outstanding example of someone called to the nations. He has a good ear for language and passion for church building and missions. When our culture is so devoid of youth who go full time into world missions in such a great hour of need and possibility of harvest, Josh's book will be a good resource to pass on to someone you love...

ANGIE RUTH SCHUM
President of Psalm 91 Ministries and Crosslines Ministry
Author: God's Smuggler Jr.
Co-Author: Psalm 91 Military, Psalm 91 Teen and Psalm 91 Workbook

I enthusiastically invite you to enter the journey chronicled in this book, *Called by the Fire*. These pages carry you deeply into the story of the lives of modern-day missionaries who have stepped boldly and completely into the calling of God upon their lives. Josh and Olivia Muse have joyously laid down their lives out of their love for Jesus and their intense desire for others to know Him. The Holy Spirit has led them into many of the most dangerous and darkest places on earth to show others the love of God and the power of the Holy Spirit. I have been blessed to be a part of several of the stories in this book, and a first-hand witness to many of the miracles. I can attest to their veracity and accuracy. In sharing these stories, you are encouraged to see the goodness of God, let your faith grow stronger, and step into the Fire!

DR. DON RAGLAND
Director (with my wife, Jackie) of the Schools of Mission
and Leadership for Kaleo International
Author: *The Holy Spirit: a Layman's Perspective*

FOREWORD BY **JOHN ARNOTT**

CALLED BY THE FIRE

JOSHUA MUSE

Called by the Fire – Joshua Muse

© Copyright – Joshua Muse

All rights reserved. This book is protected by the copyright laws of the United States of America. This book may not be copied or reprinted for commercial gain or profit. The use of short quotations or occasional page copying for personal or group study is permitted and encouraged. Permission will be granted upon request.

Unless otherwise identified, Scripture quotations are from the English Standard Version. All emphasis within Scripture quotations is the author's own. Quotations marked by NIV are from the New International Version. Quotations marked by KJV are from the King James Version. Quotations marked by NKJV are from the New King James Version.

Please note that our publishing style capitalizes certain pronouns in Scripture that refer to the Father, Son, and Holy Spirit. Take note that the name satan and related names are not capitalized. We choose not to acknowledge him, even to the point of violating grammatical rules.

Edition by Karen Cota and Cheyenne Klein

Cover design and layout design by Pedro Barreto

For more information on local or foreign distributors, write to:

orders@kaleointernational.org

Or reach us on the Internet: www.kaleointernational.org

ISBN: 979-8-9856324-0-8

Printed by *Kaleo Publishing*.

For Worldwide Distribution, Printed in Mexico.

With my deepest love, I would like to dedicate this book to my wife Olivia. She has and continues to walk through fire with me. I can't think of anyone I'd rather have by my side.

To my children, you need to know that your lives are miracles of God's faithfulness. You have been consecrated and dedicated to Him! I am writing this book in large part for you, as an eye-witness to God's unfailing faithfulness! I pray that someday when you read this book it will inspire you to pursue Jesus whole heartedly! I pray this will just be the beginning of the great miracles God will do through your lives!

Deepest thanks to...

To my mother and father, thank you for leading me to Jesus all those years ago and showing me how to live for Him. Thank you for demonstrating the love of the heavenly Father to me. These miracles are part of your legacy in the Kingdom.

To my sister and brother-in-law, thank you for being my friends and always loving and praying for your brother even when his crazy ideas don't make sense.

To my mother-in-law, thank you for raising the wonderful gift that is my wife and blessing her to go to the nations with me.

To my large extended family, thank you for continuing to love us even though we are often far away.

To our Kaleo International family around the world, each of you inspire me! I am beyond honored to serve the Lord alongside such amazing heroes of the faith.

To our network of partners and supporters who have prayed and given sacrificially over the years, thank you so much for sowing into the Kingdom of God.

To our dear family and friends in Brownwood, Texas, thank you for supporting us and being our home base for many years. To my pastors and friends, Kelly and Donna Crenshaw, thank you for going with me on so many wild adventures. Kelly, you have taught me so much about the Kingdom and how to step into the realm of the impossible. To Angie Schum and Peggy Joyce Ruth, thank you for investing in discipling me during my college years. Peggy Joyce, I will always be grateful for how you and your husband Jack invested in this stubborn, headstrong college student all those years ago.

To our family in Iris Global, thank you for the open heaven that I encountered during my times with you in Mozambique. Heidi and Rolland Baker, thank you for setting such an example for all of us of what it means to live a life laid down. To Pamela and Tony Maxwell, thank you for believing in us and calling us higher.

To all of our Catch the Fire Partners family associated with the Toronto Revival, thank you for receiving us and loving us even when we were broken. To John and Carol Arnott, thank you for believing in us and making so many trips to Mexico to help us press in for revival. To Dan and Gwen Slade, thank you for finding us in Mozambique and believing in the call of God on our lives during one of the hardest seasons of our ministry. Duncan and Kate Smith, thank you for investing in us and revival in Mexico! And to so many others from this amazing network who have prayed for us and supported our work around the world.

To our dear friends Tineke Bouwman, Cameron Wright, and John Peña (just to name a few), thank you for introducing us to another level of the supernatural manifestations of the Holy Spirit! We are so grateful for the five-fold ministry impact you continue to have on our Kaleo family!

To Karen Cota and her staff, thank you for helping me through the process of writing, editing and publishing!

CONTENTS

	Foreword by John Arnott	19
	Introduction	21
Part 1: Called by the Lord		
1.	Surprised by God's Call	27
2.	Turning Aside	31
3.	Encountering the Fire	39
4.	Where are You at?	51
Part 2: Transformed by the Fire		
5.	Purifying Fire	65
6.	The Covenant	71
7.	The Fulfillment	83
8.	The New Beginning	93
9.	Face-to-Face with God	101
10.	Setting the Captives Free	109
Part 3: Sent to the Nations		
11.	Who is on the Throne?	123
12.	The Burning Ones	135

13.	A Dead Man	145
14.	The Fire of Testing	155
15.	The Heartbeat of the Lord	161
16.	Seeing and Perceiving	175
17.	The New Normal	189
18.	The Fire, the Plague and the Flood	199
19.	Follow the Fire	213
	Conclusion: Carriers of the Glory	227
	About Kaleo International	232

FOREWORD

I first met Josh Muse in Toronto at a Partners in Harvest Conference in 2014. I was very impressed with this young 20 something missionary who seemed to have ministry experience way beyond his years. He had already been all over the globe in various danger-filled mission fields in Africa, Asia and Latin America, and seemed to be powerfully led/driven by the fire of the Holy Spirit.

He had come from a conservative Christian background with a solid grounding in the word of God, the Bible, but had subsequently encountered the Holy Spirit in several overwhelming breakthroughs through the ministry of the Bakers in Mozambique, a Randy Clark meeting where he shook for a week under the power, and subsequent to that, in Catch The Fire Toronto where he was again powerfully touched by God. Josh and Olivia were revolutionized by these Holy Spirit rendezvous, and began their ministry of missions and church planting, touching Africa, Asia, and Mexico. Calling their ministry Kaleo, after the Greek word meaning 'called', they eventually based in Reynosa, Mexico, landing in the middle of cartel turf wars and deep poverty and needs among the precious people there. As a family, they are building a solid mission organization in Mexico as well as other nations around the world.

Called by the Fire is such an apt title for this faith-filled adventure. You will be thrilled with the stories of miracle after miracle that have paved the way for these two young world changers to have already made a global impact on the body of Christ as they plant church after church and build an amazing team of young leaders in Mexico, Africa and beyond. You will be encouraged yourself to reach for miraculous ministry as you too endeavor to bring the Kingdom of God in power and love to a very broken hurting world.

Well done, Josh and Olivia. Your life story is a very compelling witness of what young people today can accomplish for Jesus when their lives are sold out to Him. You have experienced the Glory and continue to do so. Amazing fruit will always follow that. This book is one that you cannot put down. And for you, dear reader, these pages are an invitation for you to enter into the greatest adventure of your lives.

The stage is being set for an unprecedented global move of God that will be driven by signs, miracles and wonders. God is looking for radical lovers of Jesus, willing to lay their lives down and pursue Him daily with prayer and obedience. He is calling you into the Fire of His passionate love, to be a carrier of His glory!

John Arnott
Founder, *Catch The Fire Ministries*

INTRODUCTION

It is not by accident that you are reading this book at this moment. God is calling you. But what is He calling you to do? The call and will of God for your life is not meant to be mysterious, or hidden from you. God is calling each of us, if we will choose to listen. God uses signs and wonders to get our attention. These signs serve to awaken us from complacency and shake us out of our spiritual slumber.

Once while ministering in a remote village in Honduras, we were visiting a town where they spoke a tribal language called *Garifino*. The *Garifino* people are the descendants of African slaves who escaped captivity in the Caribbean and settled in Central America. They speak a dialect which is a combination of various West African languages. Our team was walking through the dirt streets of this little village praying in tongues and asking God to open doors in the community. Suddenly, we looked behind us and saw two teenage girls come running out of a house. They started following us from a distance, staring intently. After a few minutes, they gathered their courage and came closer. We stopped and asked them in Spanish what they wanted. One of the girls said that as we passed their house, they heard me speaking in tongues and understood what I was saying. They each heard me perfectly in their own language calling them to come outside. One girl was not saved and was sick with a chronic pain in her stomach, began to say that she had heard me calling her in her language to come and be healed. The other girl was a believer. She excitedly shared that she had heard me calling her in her language to come and receive the baptism of the Holy Spirit. Both knew that God was calling them. We laid hands on the girl who needed healing and prayed and God healed her on the spot. She gave her life to Christ and fell to the ground speaking in tongues. We laid hands on the other girl and immediately the fire of God fell on her and she was baptized in the Holy Spirit and began speaking in tongues. People started to come out of the houses to see what was happening. We explained that the Holy Spirit was moving and more people came out to receive healing and give their lives to Christ.

In the same way that God called these girls to Himself, He is also calling you right now. Surrendering to the call of God requires us to be willing to step out of our comfort zone and into the fierce storm that surrounds Him. When Jesus walked on water, His disciples were afraid. What He was doing was so far beyond their comprehension that they thought He was a ghost. Peter, however, was willing to step out and follow Jesus into the unknown:

«And Peter answered him, "Lord, if it is you, command me to come to you on the water." He said, "Come." So Peter got out of the boat and walked on the water and came to Jesus» (Matthew 14:28-29).

In much the same way, God is inviting us to be willing to step out and follow Him. It is both terrifying and exhilarating to follow Jesus into the unknown realm. In our walk of faith, we find out who we were truly made to be. As we follow the call of God, we also find out who we are and who He made us to be. Within each of us is a deep desire to be part of something much bigger than ourselves. Every one of us desire to live a life of significance. We each long to serve a cause that will matter in eternity. We each cry out for a love that will bring significance to our lives. When I first heard the Lord call me, it changed the trajectory and course of my life. I could never have imagined the adventure, danger, joy and love that I would encounter as I stepped out to follow the fire of the Lord. The following stories are the accounts of the miracles I have seen God do with my own eyes and the lessons that He has taught me along the way.

I would like to invite you today to join me on this journey as we follow Jesus into the Fire.

PART 1

CALLED BY THE LORD

«Now Moses was tending the flock of Jethro his father-in-law, the priest of Midian, and he led the flock to the far side of the wilderness and came to Horeb, the mountain of God. There the angel of the LORD appeared to him in flames of fire from within a bush. Moses saw that though the bush was on fire it did not burn up. So Moses thought, "I will go over and see this strange sight——why the bush does not burn up." When the LORD saw that he had gone over to look, God called to him from within the bush:

"Moses! Moses!"

And Moses said, "Here I am."

Exodus 3:1-4, NIV

APOCALIPSIS 1:14 HIS HEAD AND HIS HAIR WERE WHITE LIKE WOOL, WHITE AS SNOW. AND **HIS EYES WERE LIKE FLAMES OF FIRE. EXODUS 3:2** THERE THE ANGEL OF THE LORD APPEARED TO HIM IN A **BLAZING FIRE FROM THE MIDDLE OF A BUSH.** MOSES STARED IN AMAZEMENT. THOUGH THE BUSH WAS ENGULFED IN FLAMES, IT DIDN'T BURN UP. **ISAIAH 4:5** THEN THE LORD WILL PROVIDE SHADE FOR MOUNT ZION AND ALL WHO ASSEMBLE THERE. HE WILL PROVIDE A CANOPY OF CLOUD DURING THE DAY AND **SMOKE AND FLAMING FIRE AT NIGHT,** COVERING THE GLORIOUS LAND. **SONG OF SONGS 8:6** PLACE ME LIKE A SEAL OVER YOUR HEART, LIKE A SEAL ON YOUR ARM. FOR LOVE IS AS STRONG AS DEATH, ITS JEALOUSY AS ENDURING AS THE GRAVE. **LOVE FLASHES LIKE FIRE, THE BRIGHTEST KIND OF FLAME. LEVITICUS 6:** REMEMBER, THE FIRE MUST BE **KEPT BURNING ON THE ALTAR AT ALL TIMES. IT MUST NEVER GO OUT. DEUTERONOMY 5:4** AT THE MOUNTAIN THE LORD SPOKE TO YOU FACE TO FACE **FROM THE HEART OF THE FIRE. PSALMS 104:4** THE WINDS ARE YOUR MESSENGERS; **FLAMES OF FIRE ARE YOUR SERVANTS. LEVITICUS 6:12** MEANWHILE, THE FIRE ON THE ALTAR **MUST BE KEPT BURNING;** IT MUST NEVER GO OUT. EACH MORNING THE PRIEST WILL ADD **FRESH WOOD TO THE FIRE AND** ARRANGE THE BURNT OFFERING ON IT. HE WILL THEN BURN THE FAT OF THE PEACE OFFERINGS ON IT. **2 KINGS 2:11** AS THEY WERE WALKING ALONG AND TALKING, SUDDENLY A **CHARIOT OF FIRE APPEARED, DRAWN BY HORSES OF FIRE.** IT DROVE BETWEEN THE TWO MEN, SEPARATING THEM, AND ELIJAH WAS CARRIED BY A WHIRLWIND INTO HEAVEN. **JEREMÍAS 20:9** BUT IF I SAY I'LL NEVER MENTION THE LORD OR SPEAK IN HIS NAME, **HIS WORD BURNS IN MY HEART LIKE A FIRE.** IT'S LIKE A FIRE IN MY BONES! I AM WORN OUT TRYING TO HOLD IT IN! I CAN'T DO **ACTS 2:3** THEN, WHAT LOOKED LIKE **FLAMES OR TONGUES OF FIRE** APPEARED AND SETTLED ON EACH OF THEM. **ACTS 2:18-19** IN THOSE

CHAPTER 1

SURPRISED BY GOD'S CALL

I grew up on a small farm in Texas; it made for a wonderful childhood. I was taught the Bible from a young age and accepted Jesus when I was 5 years old. I loved my family, I loved our farm and never imagined that I would ever leave this type of life. But then one day when I was 9 years old, I was sitting in a Sunday school class at our church as missionaries stationed in West Africa were sharing about their ministry. They told stories from the field and talked about tribes that had never heard the gospel before, about people who had never even heard the name of Jesus. Growing up in the Bible Belt, this was something new and unimaginable for me. I was shocked, and thought to myself, "Wow, someone should really go and do something about that." Immediately I heard a voice say, "My son I am going to send you. You will be a missionary. You will go around the world and take the gospel to unreached people and tribes." I was shocked to hear God's voice in this way because our church was a very conservative evangelical church which did not publicly embrace any of the charismatic gifts or teach that God could still speak openly to us today. For this reason, I really had no grid for what was happening to me. As I sat there surrounded by other kids, everything else seemed to go quiet around me as I was momentarily lost in this encounter with Jesus. I was both scared and amazed that God would choose to speak to me, so I simply said yes. I had no way of knowing what that yes would come to mean in my life, but I can tell you with absolute certainty that the course of my life was forever changed by that encounter.

There are moments in our lives when we are seeking to know God's will and other moments when God's sovereign purposes surprise us in the most profound ways. In my years of serving the Lord the most common question I get from people is, "How do I know if God is calling me?" My answer is simple and emphatic: Yes, He is calling you. But unto what purpose? That is the real question. This is a question that you can only know the answer to if you are willing to step into His fiery presence.

> Now Moses was tending the flock of Jethro his father-in-law, the priest of Midian, and he led the flock to the far side of the wilderness and came to Horeb, the mountain of God.
>
> Exodus 3:1 NIV

Moses was an interesting character with a fascinating backstory. Born as a Hebrew slave in Egypt during a time of horrific genocide against his race, he was placed in the Nile River and found and adopted by Pharaoh's daughter. He was raised in the palace as Egyptian royalty, but still deep within himself he knew who he really was. This inner turmoil of being caught between the two worlds eventually resulted in him murdering an Egyptian who was beating a Hebrew slave. Out of fear for his life, he then escaped into the desert to live out his life as a refugee. There he began a new life and career as a shepherd on the far side of the desert…what is the only thing worse than exile in the desert? Exile to the far side of the desert. Truthfully, Moses had fallen just about as far as he could in life and hit rock bottom. Little did he know that everything in his life up until that point was meant to prepare him for his assignment. When God calls a person to step into their destiny, their first stop in the process is not usually the fullness of what they are called to do. Almost always, the first step on the road to your calling is the backside of the desert. The desert seasons of our lives are part of the process of sanctification we are called to walk in. It is in these seasons that we experience the hardest clashes between our old man and new nature in Christ. The desert is the place where you must consciously choose between the works of the flesh and work of the Spirit. In the desert, you cannot hide or run but are forced to confront the reality of yourself. It is in that place of vulnerability that God Himself desires to meet you.

It has been said that hindsight is 20/20, this of course means that when we look back at our past we see more clearly. I think oftentimes, we forget that the heroes of the Bible didn't see the script in advance. Like us, they had to obey God in blind faith without knowing where they were going. In much the same way as us, most of them probably had no idea the significance of the events happening in their lives until much later. Likewise, we oftentimes fail to see the many ways in which the events of our lives have been orchestrated by God to bring us to a place to hear His voice and follow His call.

God is still calling people today, but too often we fail to hear it because our spiritual senses have become dull due to lack of use. We are constantly bombarded by the world around us. Without realizing it, we are lulled to sleep and lose sight of the great purpose for which we have been created.

It is for this reason, God chooses to set bushes on fire.

CHAPTER 2

TURNING ASIDE

When I was 16 years old, I heard the Lord speak to me again that I needed to go to Africa on a trip with my church. When I told my parents, they were understandably skeptical and questioned me about my motives. They finally concluded that I should talk to the pastor leading the trip. After visiting with him, he informed me that I was too young to go by myself and needed one of my parents to accompany me. I returned home determined to convince one of them to go with me. We argued back and forth until finally I simply prayed for God to speak. A few days later after returning home from a camping trip, my mother met me with a question, "What have you been praying?"

"That God would give you a dream or a vision about Africa," I replied.

She then began to share with me a dream that she had received a few nights before. In the dream, she saw our farm and everything our family owned being surrounded by 3 tornadoes. As the tornadoes grew closer, everything was being destroyed. The tornadoes grew nearer and nearer until she cried out to God and said, "Do you want me to go to Africa?" Immediately the tornadoes stopped and everything was restored. We both sat in silence and wept as the heaviness of this word sat upon us in the moment. A few weeks later, we found ourselves on a plane to Kenya, Africa. I arrived with stories of David Livingston in my head only to discover that the African church was far more alive and vibrant than anything I had ever encountered in the Western Hemisphere. They worshipped God with passion, prayed with faith and saw miracles. For the first time, I saw an image of the type of Christian I wanted to become. I went back to Kenya again the next year and while I was there, I met Kenyan missionaries living in South Sudan. They told us that South Sudan is hot, dry, dusty and extremely dangerous. They told stories of almost being killed in the civil war as they tried to preach the gospel. Something rose up inside me and I asked the Lord, "Can I please go help there?" Again, I heard his voice clearly say, "Yes, I will send you."

> There the angel of the LORD appeared to him in flames of fire from within a bush. Moses saw that though the bush was on fire it did not burn up. So Moses thought, "I will go over and see this strange sight - why the bush does not burn up".
>
> Exodus. 3:2-3, NIV

Moses was plodding along taking care of his sheep when suddenly he saw a marvel, a bush that was on fire but not being destroyed. The Bible says he thought to himself, "I will go over and see this strange sight—why the bush does not burn up." And when God saw that he had turned aside from the path he was walking, He decided that Moses was ready for an encounter. It has been said, "The journey of a thousand miles begins with one step." But the important question to ask is, where is that step leading you? For Moses he had to decide to turn away from his livelihood (his sheep) in order to step closer to the fire. He could be called irresponsible for neglecting his duties and leaving his sheep unattended, but his curiosity drew him closer to the fire. There is a God-given hunger in each of us to step into His fire.

In the Christian tradition in which I was raised, miracles were viewed as something that happened in the past but were not for today. While no Christian I knew denied that miracles happened in the Bible, most did not believe (or live like they believed) that it was possible to see signs and wonders in this day and age. Or if they did pray for a miracle, it was with the immediate qualifier "Your will be done." Which basically meant, "I know this probably won't happen." But these African brothers prayed in a different way; they prayed believing that things would happen and for the first time in my life I saw the Holy Spirit work in power! I knew I needed more of Him!

A short while later after graduating high school, I found a ministry who allowed me to go with them to the semi-independent, (at that time) unrecognized country of South Sudan. We were sent to go and evangelize at a town near the border with Kenya to help establish a new church plant. As the team split up to go into various villages, I went with a small group to a remote village where we were stopped by South Sudanese soldiers who were suspicious of our purposes there.

A rebel faction called the LRA (Lord's Resistance Army) had come through that area a few weeks before and killed many people. This terrorist group was originally based in Uganda but had been driven into the Congo and South Sudan by the Ugandan military. They were incredibly brutal and were led by a cult leader with a messiah complex named Joseph Kony. Kony's rebel group kidnapped children and brainwashed them into becoming child soldiers. His followers committed many atrocities throughout East and Central Africa, often massacring entire villages. They also maimed multitudes of people by cutting off their arms and legs with machetes. This terror tactic served to instill fear in the local populations of the LRA. He used a combination of traditional witchcraft and distorted Christianity to control his followers.

At this time, the LRA was being driven out of Uganda and was operating primarily in Congo and conducting raids in South Sudan. Naturally, because this group claimed to be killing in the name of God, the locals seemed to want nothing to do with Christianity. They were suspicious and almost hostile. I had no idea what to do. I was just a member of the team. The leaders had us do a prayer walk around the village. I went out with a local interpreter. I honestly did not know much about spiritual warfare so I just began to pray the words of the Lord's Prayer. The answer to my prayer came in the form of a drunken soldier. He said through my interpreter, "Khawaja (white man in Arabic), come and pray for one of my wives, she is dying." He was armed and drunk so I did not really see any other option but to go with him. We arrived at his house, a small mud and grass hut. I was shocked by what I saw as we entered: a woman laying on a grass mat naked, dying of what we were told was meningitis. Her eyes were open but glazed over and although she was breathing it was shallow and raspy with a distinct rattle sound like she was near death. She had been burned by the witch doctors with hot irons to drive out the sickness.

I looked at this woman thinking, "What can I possibly do to help her?" My interpreter, a local pastor, indicated that we should lay hands on her. I again had no idea what to do. I had never seen a miraculous healing before in my life. As I laid my hands on her, I began to pray the words of the Lord's prayer: "Your Kingdom come, Your will be done. On earth as it is in heaven." As we knelt there praying for her with our eyes closed, she suddenly sat straight up. I was so surprised, I almost fell over! She was equally surprised to see a white man in her home. "Am I dead?" she asked. It took me a while to gather my thoughts enough to reply through the interpreter that Jesus healed her.

We shared the gospel with her, and she decided to give her life to Jesus. At that moment, her husband awoke from his drunken slumber only to find his wife, who he thought was dying, very much alive cleaning her house. "My wife is alive!" He screamed and immediately left the house to gather people to come and see what the Lord had done. As we left the house, neighbors came bringing sick children for us to pray for.

That day a church was established in their community. Soldiers who had wanted nothing to do with Jesus only a few days before began giving their lives to Christ because of the miracles Jesus was doing among them. I laid in my bed that night unable to sleep, in awe of what I had seen that day. I said to the Lord, "This is how I want to live the rest of my life—with your power."

A group of Pokot women hearing a presentation of the gospel.

Pokot women dancing and singing to welcome our team to their village.

Landing on a dirt runway near Torit, South Sudan.

Tukals: traditional rural houses in South Sudan made with grass roofs and mud walls.

Local Sudanese favorite: fried termites.

CHAPTER 3

ENCOUNTERING THE FIRE

After my trip to South Sudan, I went to visit some missionary friends in the northern part of Uganda. This ministry was different from anything I had ever encountered because there they were completely unapologetic about the move of the Holy Spirit. In those days, northern Uganda was still recovering from the civil war with the *LRA*. Revival had broken out among the believers in northern Uganda. Before the revival, the Ugandan government had been unable to defeat the rebels despite years of brutal fighting. Thousands of people fled to IDP (internally displaced people) camps as the fighting dragged on in their villages. In the midst of the chaos, God raised up revival leaders who prayed and fasted to see breakthrough in their country. The result was a sweeping victory in the north against the LRA with thousands becoming born again and many churches being planted.

While I was visiting this ministry, I stayed in the men's dormitory and was amazed at how the Christians would wake up early and begin praying loudly in another language (I thought they were speaking a tribal dialect but found out afterwards it was actually the gift of tongues). These men could pray for hours. When they prayed, they really believed that God would move, and He did! I went with them to the villages and watched them preach the gospel with signs and wonders. I saw them cast demons out of people who were oppressed and preach with a power I had never encountered before. I did not understand what was missing in my life, but I knew I needed what they had. So finally, in frustration I asked some of them, "What do you have that I don't have?" With a smile they replied, "You need the fire of the Holy Spirit."

I did not know what this fire was, but in my heart I knew I needed the Holy Spirit more than anything else in my life! "How can I receive the fire?" I asked. They then explained the baptism of the Holy Spirit. They talked about how Jesus sent the Holy Spirit at Pentecost to baptize the church with His power to give them anointing to fulfill the commission. They told me I would speak in new tongues and be baptized in the power of God. As they began to pray, I felt fire come upon me and began speaking in another language. I did not fully understand what all this meant, but I knew something had radically changed in my life. A few days after that encounter with God, I remember sitting in a church service in Uganda when a demonized woman entered and began to disrupt the service. I got out of my chair and walked over to her and with an authority I had never experienced before commanded the demon to leave. The demon shrieked and left the woman. It was in that moment, I knew that something had really changed in me.

> When the LORD saw that he had gone over to look, God called to him from within the bush, "Moses! Moses!"
>
> Exodus 3:4, NIV

You and I were made to live a life full of fire! God is waiting for us to turn aside and focus on Him! When Moses turned to face the fire of God, God Himself spoke to Moses out of the fire; calling him by name. I can only imagine how powerful a moment this was for Moses that God would call him by his name. God's call to us is very personal. He wants to touch us with His fire and speak directly to our hearts. It is interesting how fire is a recurring theme in both the Old and New Testament. In the Old Testament, fire usually means purification and calling. John the Baptist said,

> I baptize you with water. But one who is more powerful than I will come, the straps of whose sandals I am not worthy to untie. He will baptize you with the Holy Spirit and fire.
>
> Luke 3:16, NIV

This baptism in fire is one of the most transformative things that can happen in the life of a Christian. In fact, Jesus told his disciples not to go out until they had received the power of the Holy Spirit:

> Do not leave Jerusalem, but wait for the gift my Father promised, which you have heard me speak about. For John baptized with water, but in a few days, you will be baptized with the Holy Spirit.
>
> Acts 1:4-5, NIV

God is still calling us to step into his fiery presence. The baptism of the Holy Spirit is a powerful experience in the life of the believer that empowers them to fulfill God's call on their lives. After this experience with God's fire, He then invites us to follow Him into the desert. The desert seasons of our lives are crucial in the formation of our character. Jesus modeled this Himself when he was baptized by John.

> In those days Jesus came from Nazareth of Galilee and was baptized by John in the Jordan. And when he came up out of the water, immediately he saw the heavens being torn open and the Spirit descending on him like a dove. And a voice came from heaven, "You are my beloved Son; with you I am well pleased." The Spirit immediately drove him out into the wilderness.
>
> Mark 1:9-12

In this passage, Jesus was baptized in water and anointed by the Spirit of God (as signified by the dove descending from heaven). But he was not led by the Spirit directly to the pulpit or the platform but was instead taken immediately into the desert to be tested. Many believers are motivated by a "career mentality" in regard to their ministry. This mentality seeks promotion and "success" in ministry through obtaining position and salary. For this reason, many young people go to seminary hoping to encounter God and leave with a career plan for "success" in a religious system. Likewise, many pastors jump from church to church looking to see who will pay them more, or provide better benefits or opportunities. This pattern leaves us hollow and without vision. I do not have anything against ministers earning a living, I believe it's Biblical and right. However, I also believe that God desires to restore a pure zeal to His church to follow His call with great passion no matter what the cost. In order to follow Him and be used by His Spirit we must be willing to follow Him wherever He may lead. We must break free from this career mentality of ministry and learn to seek God's presence above all else; willing to follow Him into the desert and the fire.

It is important to recognize the type of desert we may find ourselves in. Sometimes we may find ourselves in a desert of our own making like Moses, who ended up there because of His own sin. Or like Jesus, we may find ourselves serving in a difficult place as an act of obedience. The only way out of the desert caused by our own actions is through repentance whereas the desert of testing requires radical obedience.

In 2007, I was sitting with a group of missionary leaders in a meeting in Dallas, Texas. They were discussing areas with the greatest need for the gospel in South Sudan. They mentioned that there was a pastor in a state called Upper Nile that had been trained in Kenya but had gone back to his people, Malakal, and no one had been to visit him. They said that the area was highly volatile because it was very remote and on the border between the north and south. I spoke up and said that I wanted to go. They looked at each other unsure if I was serious. After a few months, we were able to get in contact with the pastor and he agreed to host me on a scouting trip.

South Sudan at this time was not yet a recognized country. They had fought a brutal civil war against the northern government and after many years won their freedom. They were in the process of rebuilding their country. The capital of Juba had been hit hard by the war.

When I flew into Juba, I remember looking down from the plane and seeing the downed fighter jets and exploded tanks from the war that had simply been pushed to either side of the runway. The evidence of freshly filled-in craters from aerial bombardments were sporadically scattered across the runway. As I stepped off the plane, I saw heavily armed SPLA (Sudanese People's Liberation Army) soldiers standing guard throughout with sandbagged perimeters around strategic buildings. After passing through the chaotic immigration system, I was informed there were no flights to Malakal from Juba. In my limited Arabic, the airport staff told me that no one flew there. I stepped back from the counter feeling completely overwhelmed and alone in a country where I did not speak the language or have any friends.

As I stood there unsure what to do, a very tall Dinka man walked up to me and asked me in perfect English if I needed help. I explained the situation and he took me into the correct office and within minutes I had a flight to Malakal. I thanked him, he explained that he had been a refugee in the USA during the war and was glad to help someone from the country that had taken him in.

As I walked the streets of Juba to find a place to stay, I saw craters from the bombs that had been dropped not long ago, as well as tanks and destroyed military vehicles left in the middle of the road. Signs on the outskirts of the city warned people not to walk in certain areas that had not been swept for landmines yet. It was a surreal feeling for a small-town farm kid to walk these streets and see images that seemed straight out of National Geographic.

A few days later I was able to get on a flight to Malakal, the capital of Upper Nile state. I met the local pastor, a very tall Dinka man named John. We traveled for several hours in the back of a truck to his village called Baliet. His family was in the process of constructing a simple mud hut to be my home. The Dinka are very tall, nomadic cattle herders whose lives revolve around their cattle. Growing up on a ranch myself, I felt very at home among these amazing people. The men would spend their days in the grasslands protecting their cows. They would then bring them back to the villages at night and use the dried cow dung from the days before to start hundreds of small fires around the cows to drive away the mosquitos. This created an eerie haze over the village and left almost everyone with a perpetual cough. Although many of the Dinka in that area had converted to either Christianity or Islam, they still followed their traditional animistic religion.

After a few days of arriving in the village, I met with the Dinka tribal elders to explain my mission and purpose there. I shared the gospel with them in their dark, smoke-filled hut. After I had shared, the elders began to speak. They mocked the churches in the villages who sang songs and preached about a God of power but did not see people healed from their prayers.

One elder pointed his finger in my face and said, "When our families were sick, we took them to the churches and nothing happened. When our wives couldn't have children, we took them to the churches and they prayed but nothing happened. But when we took them to witchdoctors and made sacrifices to the spirits, we received the miracles we needed. When your God does miracles in our midst, we will choose to believe in your God instead, but until the day where your God shows His power, we will follow our traditional ways."

I felt like I did not have a good answer for them, but I replied that I had seen the power of God demonstrated in my life and I would pray and believe that they would see the power of the gospel and come to believe in Christ.

I spent the following years evangelizing and helping to multiply the churches. We started programs to take care of widows and orphans and saw the churches begin to grow with new churches planted, but there was still a problem. We knew that for people following animistic religions, being able to seeing God's power was key for their decision to convert. Oftentimes Westerners see people who follow these religions as primitive or unintelligent; however, nothing could be further from the truth. These tribal religions are complex belief systems whereby the adherent must curry favor with demon spirits to gain prestige and power in their community. Animistic people see themselves as being caught in the middle between powerful unseen forces. The religious systems are controlled by shamans and healers who function as mediums between the spirits and the people. The shamans rely on sacrifices both human (in some cultures) and animals to gain favor with the spirit realm. I have seen for myself that many of these witches are able to do miracles through the power of the spirits, but the demons are not altruistic in their motivations and always require something in return. Many powerful healers or shamans have even been required to sacrifice close family members to gain more power. In these religions, there is nothing done by the spirits that is motivated by love; everything is based on fear. Most animistic people have an understanding that there is a supreme creator God who is above all other spirits. However, most people believe that this God is distant and unknowable.

In order for them to believe, they must encounter a supernatural love that has the power to set them free from their oppression. In the past missionaries have tried to "educate" the animism out of tribal people or even prohibit (in colonial days) their practices. These actions may have caused outward compliance but still left people bound in fear of spiritual forces because they did not encounter the power of Jesus to set them free. As I became more acquainted with the local churches, I saw that in this void of power many "Christians" would also seek the help of witches and traditional healers. There was so much confusion because of the belief that God was distant and unknowable. In much of the Western world, people are often ignorant of the spiritual world and do not believe that demons even exist. Unfortunately, Western missionaries are often trying to convert animistic people to Westernism rather than true Christianity. I saw this play out before and did not want to make their same mistake. Much of the New Testament was written to people bound in animistic religion and spiritism. It was to people like this that the Apostle Paul wrote:

> And my speech and my message were not in plausible words of wisdom, but in demonstration of the Spirit and of power, so that your faith might not rest in the wisdom of men but in the power of God.
>
> I Corinthians. 2:4-5

I continued serving in that region of South Sudan for about 5 years. I continued traveling back and forth as well as making trips to other nations. I learned their culture and how to communicate the basics of the gospel in their language. I prayed and fasted for an awakening in the church that would impact the community. This time in South Sudan was incredibly powerful for my spiritual growth; it was better training for me than any seminary I could have attended. It was there that I learned to teach and preach, and how to fast and seek God. I began to pray for the sick but did not see any verifiable healing miracles despite praying for hundreds of people. This country was harsh and rugged and at the same time beautiful and majestic. It was an unforgiving and volatile land that constantly teetered on the verge of war. It was in this desert that I feel I really learned what it means to seek God.

Once while sitting in my hut, the Lord spoke to me to return to the USA and study. He told me that there was a new season of training and preparation coming to prepare me for what he had for me to do. I wept as I heard these words. I wanted to spend the rest of my life in a place like this and felt that time in the West would be time wasted in my life. But I decided to obey. The Lord opened the door wide for me to study during this season and provided a full scholarship to a university in central Texas called Howard Payne. During that time, I continued doing ministry whenever I had the opportunity. Every break I would travel back to South Sudan and other nations to minister and share the gospel.

During the LRA wars, most northern Ugandans fled their villages in the "bush" and came together in massive IDP camps where there was a certain degree of protection from the rebels. These camps became epicenters for the revival that swept across the northern part of the country.

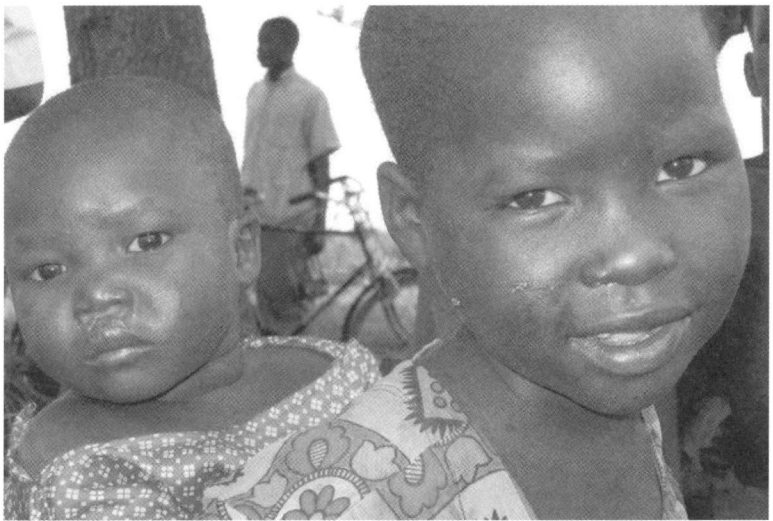

In the IDP camps, it was common for the oldest daughters, often just small children themselves, to take care of their younger siblings while their parents worked their crops outside the camps.

The Dinka are a tall nomadic people who are the largest tribe in South Sudan. Before the war, the men typically led their large herds of cattle through remote areas for grazing. Because of the war, most nomadic people lost their herds and subsequently their way of life.

In Dinka society, villages are led by elders and chiefs who are responsible for the cultural and spiritual direction of their villages.

In many remote regions in Africa vehicles are unreliable because it is impossible to obtain replacement parts so old-fashioned transport is sometimes the best option.

CHAPTER 4

WHERE ARE YOU AT?

After being baptized in the Holy Spirit, I was incredibly hungry to be trained how to walk in the Spirit. While studying at Brownwood, Texas, I felt very alone. I didn't know any Americans who really walked in the power of the Holy Spirit as the Africans did. While studying for my undergraduate degree I met a group of charismatic college students who would meet in a coffee shop on the campus of Howard Payne University called *Crosslines*. I was so excited to meet people who could help me understand the Biblical basis for the experiences I had been having with the Holy Spirit. I never had the opportunity to be intentionally discipled by believers who were filled with the Holy Spirit and who valued so much both the power of the Spirit and the stability of the Word of God.

After being a part of this ministry for a few months, I was invited to go to a revival meeting at a large Baptist church in Abilene,

Texas. A man named Randy Clark was speaking that night. Randy had been instrumental in helping birth multiple revivals around the world. However, I had read lots of negative things online that made me nervous. I arrived with a small group from my school and sat toward the back (in case things got too crazy). As the worship began, I saw people laying on the ground shaking, while others were laughing and others were singing and dancing. Then when Randy began to minister, things started to get even crazier. He called out words of knowledge and people were being healed. He began to talk about the anointing of God and impartation. I was touched by his message but was also freaked out by what was going on around me. I began to judge the people who were laughing and shaking. I even questioned if what they were doing was demonic or from the Holy Spirit. However, as soon as that thought crossed my mind, I felt something like electricity go through my hands and arms. As I looked down at my hands, I was shocked to see them shaking uncontrollably. I became afraid as I felt the electricity surge through my entire body and couldn't stop shaking.

Suddenly I heard the Holy Spirit speak to me saying, "This is not a demon. This is Me."

"What are you doing then Lord?" I asked.

"You have become hard, dry and religious and I am shaking that out of you tonight," came the reply.

About that time Randy began to call anyone who was being touched by the Holy Spirit to come to the front for an impartation. I could barely walk but set off to the front. I do not remember much of what happened that night but in that encounter with the Holy Spirit, I know that I was delivered from a religious spirit that had caused me to doubt the Lord for many years. That night represented a tipping point in my walk with the Holy Spirit. My hunger for God overcame my fear of the unknown. I was radically touched by God's presence that night and didn't stop shaking for a week.

...And Moses said, "Here I am"...

Exodus 3:4, NIV

Where are You at?

In Genesis 3, Adam and Eve sinned against God and the Bible says that their eyes were opened to understand the evil of sin. Their actions set in motion a downward spiral in their relationship with God that each of us as their descendants have continued on through the generations. They saw what they had done, so they ran and hid from God. When God came to them, he called to them saying, "Adam where are you?" Now, obviously God knew exactly where Adam was, nothing we can do will every catch Him by surprise. However, the reason God called out to Adam was so that Adam would have to take into account where his actions had led him.

When my son Caleb was a toddler, he did not like to stop playing long enough to have his diaper changed. So in order to avoid this horrible fate of having to get a new diaper, he would hide under the table. Everyone in the house could smell that something was wrong, but he continued to hide his filth. I knew exactly where he was. He was not hidden from me, but he was only prolonging the process by hiding away. In many ways, this is how we act in our relationship with God. Human nature since the fall of Adam has been to hide and conceal our sin, faults and mistakes. God does not hunt us down to drag us back to Him. Instead, He calls to us, like He did to Adam, like He did to Moses, and invites us to come to Him as an act of our own free will.

Once while I was flying through the Juba airport, the capital of South Sudan, I arrived only to discover that my connecting flight had been cancelled. I was very frustrated but eventually was able to book another flight for the following day. The next day as I entered through customs, I saw a Chinese man sitting in the waiting area. I sat down near him and greeted him in Mandarin. He was surprised and happy to hear a familiar greeting. After explaining that I only knew a few words, we switched to English and I began to share the gospel. He shook his head in disbelief. He chuckled as he went on to tell me that his mother was a Christian and had been trying for years to get him to accept Jesus. He left his home hoping to escape the constant barrage only to find himself sitting next to pastors and missionaries almost everywhere he went. We continued talking for a few more minutes and I told him to pay attention because God was speaking to him. A few months later, I found myself traveling through the same airport and again found myself sitting beside the same man who had been working in a completely different part of the country and was now on his way back to China. He looked at me in disbelief. "God is chasing after you, my friend. It's time to stop running," I told him. He finally relented and decided that he would follow Christ.

Following God is not easy, it requires sacrifice, but not the sacrifice that we often think of. Jesus already sacrificed everything for us so that we could receive our salvation as a free gift, not out of good works but from His grace. There is truly nothing we can do to earn His gift. Most of the things Jesus asks us to surrender are the very things that are destroying us. The beauty of the gospel is that it is a great exchange: He gives us His life and we receive salvation, but we must in turn give to Him our sin, addiction, sickness and shame. In this way we lose nothing when we turn from sin and gain everything by following Jesus! However, once you are saved, making the decision to follow after Christ as His disciple requires us to turn away and give up the things we may think to be very important. But in reality, the things He may ask us to give up are things that are temporal and will not last in eternity. When Jesus calls us to come closer to His fire it may cost us. Stepping into His call may cost your career, relationships, plans, wealth, and reputation.

During my time in the USA, I met a young lady from my hometown and fell in love. We both thought we would get married and began to make plans for our future together. Yet every time I asked the Lord, I would immediately hear both yes and no at the same moment. This thoroughly confused me, but I chalked it up to cold feet and stress. After all, she seemed perfect. We were part of the same ministry and she said she was called to missions. I convinced myself that all was well! We both went on a mission trip with our college ministry to the Philippines. This trip was an intense introduction into missions. The Philippines is a beautiful country and the churches we worked with were filled with the power of the Holy

Spirit. The pastors who hosted us had an intense prayer life that humbled us and a passion to share the gospel and pray for the sick that I had never encountered.

Every morning, they would meet in the church where we stayed and begin praying at 5am. We would join them in prayer and together pray in tongues for several hours seeking the presence of God. After a few hours of this intense prayer, we would go out and begin street ministry. We would usually finish our days with open air crusades, and most days we would not get to sleep until 1am. It was an intense boot camp schedule meant to build our faith as well as our endurance. During this time we saw God do many incredible miracles.

One evening our team traveled to a remote island. We were interceding and preparing for an evangelistic event that night at a local park. During prayer, the Lord spoke a word to me that tonight the impossible would be possible. I was very excited about the word and as we started the event, I was continually looking around for the impossible thing that Jesus was going to do. After the message we began to pray for the sick. A woman came forward carrying a young boy. She asked us to pray for her back, but as we prayed, we saw there was something wrong with the boy. She shared with us that he had been born with cerebral palsy and had never been able to walk. We asked her if we could pray for him. She said yes and put him on the ground while she stood behind him holding him up. We gathered around and began to pray for him. After about 15 minutes he began to cry because his little legs were very unstable and he wanted his mother to pick him back up. The mother also wanted to go home but we persisted. After about 30 minutes the local pastors were telling us we needed to go and to wrap it up. We were about to stop praying when one of the American girls on the team shared that the Lord was asking her if we were willing to persevere in prayer. We all said yes, and continued praying for the little boy when suddenly, after nearly an hour of praying, the boy's ankle straightened out and he took a step. Then the other ankle straightened out and he took another step. His surprised mother let go of him and he began to walk for the first time in his life. After looking around and realizing that he was walking on his own, he began to run full speed around the basketball court, and then up and down the bleachers. His mother sat down in complete shock at what she was seeing. She began to weep uncontrollably and gave her life to Jesus after seeing this miracle that forever changed the life of her son.

During this time, I came to understand more than ever before the direct connection between Spirit-filled intercession and miracles. As well as the need for us to persevere in prayer until we see the breakthrough.

The intensity of the trip also helped me tremendously because it became obvious to me that the young lady I was going to marry was not suited for a life of foreign missions. She could not handle the food, cultural differences, or intensity of the ministry. I did not know what to do. I was in love but knew deep down in my heart that she did not share my calling. I returned home and fasted and prayed. I had one burning question…could I marry her or not? During that time, I heard the voice of the Lord clearly. He said to me, yes, I could marry her but I needed to know that if I did, I would never fulfill the calling He had for me. This was incredibly hard to hear because I was in love, but the fear of the Lord compelled me to choose His plan for my life instead of my own. The next day, I met with her and ended our relationship. It was incredibly hard, but I knew I had to do this in order to fulfill my call.

God is constantly calling us but many times the circumstances of our lives distract us from His voice and leave us confused about His nature and purpose. God will not simply yell louder than your own heart, but He will use the situations of life to get our attention and push us toward encountering the One who can change us. Moses' actions had led him to the desert, but God's sovereignty and goodness led him to the fire. Moses saw a sign, a burning bush, that caught his attention. People often ask me, "Why does God do miracles?" My answer is simple, God wants to get our attention so that we can know and experience His presence and love and be transformed. The signs point us to someone!

Where are You at?

In 2010 while I was at university, I began to gather with a small group of men to pray at 6 am. During one of these mornings someone said that we needed to pray for the city of Juarez because the violence was out of control. He read to us an article about how the previous police chiefs, in a town just outside of Juarez, called Praxedis, had been executed by the cartel. After these brutal murders, no one wanted the job. A young lady from Juarez who was a recent college graduate had stepped up and accepted the job. The person writing the article did not expect her to live very long before she was killed by the cartel. After the prayer meeting, I met with one of my good friends who also felt he needed to go and we decided that we needed to make a trip to Praxedis and share the gospel with the police chief. That Friday after class, we set out to Juarez. As we drove the 9 hours from Brownwood to El Paso, we continued to read more about the city we were headed to. At that time, Juarez was ranked as one of the most violent cities in the world with an average of eleven murders a day. I reached out to a contact I knew from a short mission trip I had made there many years before. We arrived and found our way to the police station in Praxedis. We parked in front of the building and as we walked up, we saw the doors barricaded with thick iron sheets bolted to the walls to cover the windows. Sandbags were in front of the doors and we could see the glint of a number of rifles through the holes in the walls. A police woman in heavy body armor met us at the entrance and asked us what we wanted. We have come to pray for you was our reply. The lady was shocked but invited us in. We began to share the gospel with her and the others. Several of them were openly weeping. We gave them Bibles and prayed for them. As we left, one of the police officers stopped us and with tears in her eyes asked us to please not forget about them and not to forget about their city. With those words ringing in our ears, we knew that God was opening up a door of opportunity into this region.

The ministry I was a part of in Brownwood, Texas had released a powerful book based on Psalm 91. This book was a powerful revelation to me of God's covenant of protection for the believer. It had been translated into Spanish. We decided to go back to Juarez and take several hundred copies of this book to give out to the Juarez police along with Bibles. At that time, Ciudad Juarez was under martial law because of the infighting between the cartels. All the fighting was to get control over the smuggling routes. Kidnapping, extortion and murder had become the norm. The military had been sent in to take control of the city. Many of the local police had been killed or kidnapped and those that remained of the local police were either terrified of being killed or were corrupt themselves. We pulled into one of the state police stations and asked to see their commander. Much to our surprise, the police agreed and brought us into his office. We explained that we wanted to give this book to every federal, state and local policeman as well as the soldiers in the city and share the gospel with them. He seemed amazed and was very open to prayer. He agreed to work on it, and called us a few days later saying he had made a plan and consulted with his superiors. We could share at shift change with every station in the city. Over the next few years, the Lord continued to open the door to minister to the police and army. Thanks to the generosity of one donor, we were able to put Psalm 91 books and Bibles into the hands of every policeman and most of the soldiers working in the city and saw many thousands of them pray to accept Jesus as Savior. We also began to mobilize area churches to do outreaches and saw thousands of people come to the Lord.

During that time, I was serving as a missions pastor for a local church in Brownwood. We would take teams of people to Juarez. Our church was not a large or "wealthy" church but was filled with love and the fire of the Holy Spirit. We all worked hard to raise money to do missions by trimming trees, doing lawn work and selling food and baked goods. On one trip to Juarez, we had raised $2,800 to cover the expenses of our team. On the day we left Brownwood, we purchased supplies, filled our big 15 passenger vans up with gas and purchased our team's food for the week. We spent $700 getting everything together and spent another $100 on fuel the next day on the road. When we arrived in Mexico our team secretary Steve called us into the office of the building where we were staying.

"There's something wrong with the money," he said. "I counted it 3 times since I got here and it doesn't make sense." I know for sure we had $2,800 before we bought the supplies and I have $800 in receipts but now there is $3300. This bag has not been out of my sight. I have no idea where this came from!"

We counted the money again and sure enough it was true. Over the next week, we continued to see God multiply this money supernaturally. We blessed a number of ministries and local churches and bought food to help orphanages and feed the poor. At the end of the week, we had $4,500 USD in receipts and still had $300 USD of the original money.

Once when I was a child on our family ranch, we were burning trash in the field and a strong wind swept the fire into the neighboring grass. The fire spread despite our best efforts to put it out and burned several acres of field before the firefighters could come and put it out. I remember looking at how barren and devastated the field looked immediately following the fire. However, in just a few months those fields that had burned were greener than any of the other fields. In much the same way, the fire of God brings supernatural multiplication to every area of our lives.

Part of our team who prayed for this little boy. He was completely healed of cerebral palsy. After receiving his miracle, he could walk, run and climb stairs. His mother testified that he had never walked by himself before.

Ciudad Juárez, Mexico.

Where are You at?

Over the years we have been able to share the gospel with thousands of local, state and federal police throughout Mexico and have seen many make decisions to follow Jesus.

Giving Psalm 91 books to police during the height of the violence in Juarez.

We were allowed to minister to the police during shift change in the early morning hours.

PART 2

TRANSFORMED BY THE FIRE

"Do not come any closer," God said. "Take off your sandals, for the place where you are standing is holy ground."

Then he said, "I am the God of your father, the God of Abraham, the God of Isaac and the God of Jacob." At this, Moses hid his face, because he was afraid to look at God. The LORD said, "I have indeed seen the misery of my people in Egypt. I have heard them crying out because of their slave drivers, and I am concerned about their suffering."

Exodus 3:5-7 NIV

APOCALIPSIS 1:14 HIS HEAD AND HIS HAIR WERE WHITE LIKE WOOL, WHITE AS SNOW. AND **HIS EYES WERE LIKE FLAMES OF FIRE. EXODUS 3:2** THERE THE ANGEL OF THE LORD APPEARED TO HIM IN A **BLAZING FIRE FROM THE MIDDLE OF A BUSH.** MOSES STARED IN AMAZEMENT. THOUGH THE BUSH WAS ENGULFED IN FLAMES, IT DIDN'T BURN UP. **ISAIAH 4:5** THEN THE LORD WILL PROVIDE SHADE FOR MOUNT ZION AND ALL WHO ASSEMBLE THERE. HE WILL PROVIDE A CANOPY OF CLOUD DURING THE DAY AND **SMOKE AND FLAMING FIRE AT NIGHT,** COVERING THE GLORIOUS LAND. **SONG OF SONGS 8:6** PLACE ME LIKE A SEAL OVER YOUR HEART, LIKE A SEAL ON YOUR ARM. FOR LOVE IS AS STRONG AS DEATH, ITS JEALOUSY AS ENDURING AS THE GRAVE. LOVE FLASHES LIKE FIRE, THE BRIGHTEST KIND OF FLAME. **LEVITICUS 6:13** REMEMBER, THE FIRE MUST BE **KEPT BURNING ON THE ALTAR** AT ALL TIMES. IT MUST NEVER GO OUT. **DEUTERONOMY 5:4** AT THE MOUNTAIN THE LORD SPOKE TO YOU FACE TO FACE **FROM THE HEART OF THE FIRE. PSALMS 104:4** THE WINDS ARE YOUR MESSENGERS; **FLAMES OF FIRE ARE YOUR SERVANTS. LEVITICUS 6:12** MEANWHILE, THE FIRE ON THE ALTAR **MUST BE KEPT BURNING;** IT MUST NEVER GO OUT. EACH MORNING THE PRIEST WILL ADD **FRESH WOOD TO THE FIRE** AND ARRANGE THE BURNT OFFERING ON IT. HE WILL THEN BURN THE FAT OF THE PEACE OFFERINGS ON IT. **2 KINGS 2:11** AS THEY WERE WALKING ALONG AND TALKING, SUDDENLY A **CHARIOT OF FIRE APPEARED, DRAWN BY HORSES OF FIRE.** IT DROVE BETWEEN THE TWO MEN, SEPARATING THEM, AND ELIJAH WAS CARRIED BY A WHIRLWIND INTO HEAVEN. **JEREMÍAS 20:9** BUT IF I SAY I'LL NEVER MENTION THE LORD OR SPEAK IN HIS NAME, **HIS WORD BURNS IN MY HEART LIKE A FIRE.** IT'S LIKE A FIRE IN MY BONES! I AM WORN OUT TRYING TO HOLD IT IN! I CAN'T DO IT! **ACTS 2:3** THEN, WHAT LOOKED LIKE **FLAMES OR TONGUES OF FIRE** APPEARED AND SETTLED ON EACH OF THEM. **ACTS 2:18-19** IN THOSE DAYS I WILL POUR OUT MY SPIRIT EVEN ON MY SERVANTS—MEN AND

CHAPTER 5

PURIFYING FIRE

I began to research modern revival and was amazed to hear stories about moves of God in Mozambique, Toronto, and Asia, where the Holy Spirit was crashing in on a scale I had only read about in books. Out of these revivals thousands of churches were being planted. I wanted to experience this. I had the opportunity to go to Taiwan as part of Randy Clark's ministry team to conduct an event in a stadium. I was so excited to learn how to do miracles and minister more effectively. On the first night in the country before the event started, Randy called in the team that had come from all over the world and asked to pray an impartation for us. We all lined up and he and his pastoral team came and laid their hands on our heads and prayed. I felt electricity come into my body as I fell back onto the floor. As I laid on the ground, I felt an intense heat all over my body. I also felt a heavy presence pushing me down. As hard as I tried, I could not get up off the ground, nor could I open my eyes. As I laid there shaking under this intense pressure, I became genuinely afraid. I did not know how much more of this my body could handle. In that place of the intense glory of God, I was intensely aware of my own failures and sin. The pressure, heat, and sensation of electricity all seemed to be too much. I was truly terrified, to the point where I began to wonder if I might actually be dying.

I said to the Lord, "Please stop, this is too much, I am going to die!"

I heard clearly the voice of the Lord say, "Good, I need you dead. Because unless you die, I cannot and I will not use you."

I realized in that moment that what needed to die was my old selfishness. I was faced with a choice to fight against the Lord in the battle of my flesh or to fight with Him in killing my old man. I surrendered to the Lord and cried out to Him to kill whatever in me needed to die in order for me to come closer to His glory. I do not remember how long I was on the ground, but when I got up I knew that something had radically changed in my life.

> "Do not come any closer," God said. "Take off your sandals,
> for the place where you are standing is holy ground."
>
> Exodus 3:5, NIV

Moses had walked through a lot in his lifetime. Figuratively speaking he had also worn many different types of shoes: the shoes of a slave, the shoes of a prince of Egypt, the shoes of murderer, the tattered shoes of a fugitive, and lastly the shoes of a shepherd. Like each of us Moses was carrying a lot of baggage from the things he had walked through. God speaks to Moses and says, "Do not come any closer until you take off your shoes, for the place where you are standing is holy ground." In Middle Eastern culture in the days of Moses the bottom of the feet were considered the most unclean part of the body. What God was speaking to Moses was this, in order to be consecrated to the Lord he had to take off what he had walked through in the previous seasons of his life. He had to put behind him everything of his past in order to step closer to the fiery presence of God.

Purifying Fire

As we draw near to God, He begins to strip things away from us; leaving us with a choice to turn and run away or draw nearer still. A.W. Tozer once said, "If the Holy Spirit was withdrawn from the church today, 95 percent of what we do would go on and no one would know the difference. If the Holy Spirit had been withdrawn from the New Testament church, 95 percent of what they did would stop, and everybody would know the difference." We often wonder in the church why people don't ever seem to change. The answer to this is simple…you need fire in order to make things change.

In the height of the drug war in Juarez, Mexico we conducted a pastors' conference. We had leaders from a number of different denominations in attendance. As the conference was getting started, some people came in pushing a woman in a wheelchair. Kelly Crenshaw and I began to pray for her and after a few minutes of prayer she suddenly jumped out of her wheelchair and stood to her feet. She began to walk timidly at first and then with confidence. She walked into the sanctuary, leaving us and her family standing beside her wheelchair. The family was weeping and we were confused. Her daughter regained her composure enough to explain that her mother had lost her ability to walk quite some time ago due to an unknown neurological disease. She could only get out of her chair with multiple people supporting her, and suddenly in front of everyone she was walking on her own!

Church without the presence of the Holy Spirit is like trying to cook food on a stove that has no flame or like trying to drive a car with no engine. We need the Holy Fire of His presence to burn away all that is ungodly so that we can become more like him.

John (or Pop, as everyone called him) was part of the church I attended while I went to university in Brownwood, Texas. He had been homeless for many years. It all started when he was in a severe car accident that broke his back in three places leaving him in near constant pain. This led to substance abuse and eventually left him homeless and alone. Fortunately, he did find a family and home at New Beginnings Church in Brownwood. The pastor gave him a place to stay and a chance to start over. One night I had come back from

Mexico to preach at the church. John came up to the front to receive prayer and pastor Kelly and I laid hands on his back. As we prayed for him, his back suddenly began to crack and pop as he felt something like fire go up his spine. He was amazed because for the first time since his accident he felt no pain. He began to bend over and move around and was shocked because no matter how he moved he didn't feel any pain. The pain left completely and his back was restored.

As Moses drew closer to God, he was forced to leave his old shoes behind. If you think about it, shoes carry all that we walk through. Growing up on a farm we had a house rule, take your shoes off before you come in the house (I think the reasons are self-explanatory). In the same way, our life in this world, both before and after Christ, also leaves its "dirt" on us which must be washed clean by the blood of Jesus. This happens at our salvation, but the closer we grow to Him the more things we discover in our lives and character that need to burn away. God took Moses out of Egypt and into the desert so he could then take Egypt out of the heart of Moses. However, the desert alone does not have the power to remove Egypt from our heart—the desert without His presence is just sand. It is His very presence working in our lives that causes our hearts to change the closer we draw to Him.

Many times, people think that they must clean up their lives in order to come to God. This thought is utterly absurd not to mention impossible. This would be like a sick person deciding he must get well before he could go see the doctor. The Bible says while we were still sinners, Christ died for us. This verse means that despite our sins and failures, Christ made a way for us to come to Him. And as we come to Him, He does the work to heal us and clean us up. This is the process of the fire.

During one of our ministry trips to Ciudad Juarez, a drunk man walked into our meeting. He was out of his mind on drugs and alcohol and came into the meeting talking incoherently. He had a very evil look about him and we all began to pray because we did not know what his motive in being there was. Our team ministered in the service and during the altar call he came to the front to receive prayer. As I prayed for him, I put my hand on his head.

"Ahh!" he yelled. "Your hand is hot."

"Good." I replied as I kept praying for him.

He began to weep uncontrollably, saying in Spanish. "I don't want to be a *sicario* (hired assassin) anymore. I don't want to kill anymore!" He then went on to show us his tattoos representing how many people he had murdered. He wept saying that he was tormented every night by their faces in his dreams. I looked at him and said, "Jesus can set you free."

"No!" he screamed in a demonic voice.

As I looked into his eyes, I knew that I was speaking to a demon at that moment. He then reached into his pocket, probably to grab a weapon, and I reached out my hand to put it on his head again, commanding the demon to be silent in Jesus' name. Before my hand could touch the man, he suddenly flew backwards as the power of God touched him. He fell to the ground screaming, but no matter how hard he tried to get up he couldn't. He swung his fists at us but couldn't even lift his elbows off the ground. He tried to kick us but couldn't move his legs. "How are you doing this?" he screamed. We then cast the demons out of the man. After the last demon had left him, he was able to sit up. He sat there in his right mind and sober. He had no idea how he had gotten on the floor. I then led him to Jesus. After deciding to follow Christ, he was able to stand up on his feet. His face changed completely and while the worship music played, he began to dance before the Lord!

When God chooses to manifest Himself in our lives, it is impossible to remain the same. His holy fire can completely change us and thoroughly ruin the plans of the devil for our lives. Jesus said,

> "Whoever tries to keep their life will lose it, and whoever loses their life will preserve it."
>
> Luke 17:33

The reality of heaven is that when we seek our own way, we lose our lives no matter how hard we work to preserve them. It doesn't matter how fit and healthy you may be, death is inevitable for us all. I believe one of the greatest fears for a human being is that our lives won't count for anything. For that reason, men have conquered and built fortunes, empires and nations only to discover at the end of life, it all meant nothing apart from knowing God. The great paradox of the Kingdom is this, the more you are willing to lose yourself and follow Jesus the more you will find your true self in Him. Our calling first and foremost is one of knowing and being known. As we lose ourselves in Him, he sets our lives ablaze with His glory in order to make Himself known! In that blaze of His presence and glory, we find our calling and our lives will never be the same! As God called Moses, He declared over him three aspects of His nature. In order for Moses to walk the path God had for him, it was crucial for him to understand who this God truly was. He said, "I am the God of Abraham." In order for Moses to stand against the might of Egypt, he needed to be reminded of the covenant that had been made long before between God and Abraham.

CHAPTER 6

THE COVENANT

In 2011, I was a part of a mission team from our college ministry to the Balkan region of Eastern Europe. Our team spent three weeks doing street ministry and working with local churches. During that time, I met Olivia. She is an occupational therapist who I had met before on another mission trip, but suddenly it was as if I was seeing her for the first time. I was amazed at her hunger for God and willingness to obey Him. I prayed and asked the Lord if I could pursue her, and much to my surprise he said yes. I asked again, sure that I had heard wrong, but again I heard him say yes. When we returned to the USA, I asked her out. On our first date we talked plainly and I told her I was called to serve as a missionary in warzones and unreached places and did not want to lead her on. If she felt called to that kind of life then we should go on another date. If not, it was better just to end as friends. This shocked her, but she replied that she had thought it through before coming on this date and understood what it might mean. A few months later she went to South Sudan and spent a month with a doctor friend named Norma who had been a spiritual mom to me for many years. During this time in the bush, God confirmed Olivia's call and when she returned to the USA, she informed me that she would be going on the mission field with or without me. I knew at that moment that she was meant to be my wife!

> Then he said, "I am the God of your father, the God of Abraham..."
>
> Exodus 3:6, NIV

When God told Moses who He was, He spoke saying that He was the God of Abraham, Isaac and Jacob. Each one of these men represented a different step in God's plan of redemption for mankind. I believe that God was also speaking to Moses on a deeply personal level through the lives of each of these men. He was speaking to Moses the slave, Moses the prince of Egypt, Moses the murderer, and Moses the refugee. The purpose of God in this moment was to minister to Moses on each of these levels to bring him healing and restoration so that he could step into his true calling as the liberator of Israel. God started with Abraham to remind Moses that his true identity was not as a slave. A slave has no rights, no promise, and no covenant. With this phrase, God took Moses back to remind him of His covenant with the people of Israel. Abraham lived a simple and deeply profound life of faith. His faith in God was uncomplicated; he simply believed and followed this God who had revealed Himself to him. Abraham's walk of faith led him through some dark and difficult seasons. He was tested in every way. In some areas he failed, but God deeply loved Abraham and walked with Him as a friend. God promised Abraham that although he had no children, He would make of him a mighty nation.

> The angel of the Lord called to Abraham from heaven a second time and said, "I swear by myself, declares the Lord, that because you have done this and have not withheld your son,

The Covenant

your only son, I will surely bless you and make your descendants as numerous as the stars in the sky and as the sand on the seashore. Your descendants will take possession of the cities of their enemies, and through your offspring all nations on earth will be blessed, because you have obeyed me."

Genesis 22:15-18, NIV

He waited years for this promise to be fulfilled and God was faithful to His word! Sarah, his barren wife, gave birth to a son. Isaac was born! The promise had been fulfilled! But there was just one more thing—Abraham was commanded to take this promise and sacrifice it on the altar. As a father myself, I cannot fathom how difficult it was for Abraham to agree to this unimaginable sacrifice. His relationship with God was tested like never before, but in faith Abraham believed God and laid his son on the altar. As he raised the knife, the Lord stopped Abraham and declared a covenant with him based not on Abraham's sacrifice but upon God Himself. This covenant was a promise that one day God the Father would give His own son as a sacrifice, that one day Jesus would stand in that gap as the Son of God and Son of Abraham and die to make atonement for the sins of the world. The Lord promised Abraham that his descendants would be numerous and conquer their enemies and that his offspring would one day bless all the nations of the earth. So powerful was this promise that to this day the Jewish people have survived and prevailed against unimaginable persecution. The word used for descendant is *seed*. The apostle Paul later on explains the depth of this promise:

> The promises were spoken to Abraham and to his seed. Scripture does not say "and to seeds," meaning many people, but "and to your seed," meaning one person, who is Christ.
>
> Galatians 3:16, NIV

This promise was fulfilled at the cross and has continued to bear fruit for the past 2000 years. Every day, people from different nations, tribes and tongues are entering into covenant with the God of Abraham through the Son Jesus! However, in the moment when God spoke to Moses, the descendants of Abraham were not walking in their promise, but living as slaves in Egypt. Many of us do not feel worthy of stepping into our callings because we have lived so long as slaves to the world. When you are a slave to sin, you have lost your identity; you are an orphan. It is for that reason God sent Jesus as the fulfillment of our covenant. Throughout the years God continued to rescue and redeem the people of Israel not based on their condition or obedience, but based upon the covenant that had been established. God is a God of covenant. When we find ourselves far away from our destiny and purpose in Christ, we must look back to the covenant. In that covenant, we find the blueprint to our true identity and destiny in Him.

Perhaps like Moses, you feel that you have been forgotten by God and that your promises remain unfulfilled. The Holy Spirit is here to remind you of the promise of God made available through the son Jesus Christ. In many parts of the world, people have not heard the gospel simply because they have never met a Christian before who speaks their language.

Over the years I have had the privilege of traveling to many nations sharing the gospel and helping to establish churches. In 2009, I was traveling through several countries in Asia for ministry. I was invited by a local ministry team to accompany them to an unreached village controlled by radicals from a different religion. As we arrived, they cautioned me, "Be careful not to preach here. They stone people in this region for trying to convert people to Christianity." As we arrived a crowd gathered, curious as to why a tall American was in their remote little village. The plan was to strike up conversations that would potentially lead to opportunities to share the gospel one on one.

I began to ask them about their village and what problems they were facing. They shared about how they'd been in a drought and did not get enough rain for their crops or animals. I saw an opportunity for God to do a miracle so I began to share about a time in an area of the USA where I lived when we faced a drought and we prayed for Jesus to bring rain. One man stood up and rebuked me, saying I was surely trying to convert his people with this kind of talk. The others around him yelled at him to be quiet as they wanted to hear what I had to say. I shared about the God who has power to bring the rain and that I would pray to this God for rain to come to their region.

We finished the conversation without incident. But as everyone began to walk back to their homes, another man walked up to me and began to share what had happened to him with the help of a local interpreter. He was very devout in his religion, like everyone else in his family and village. One day almost 10 years ago he became very sick. He prayed to every god he could think of, but none of them could bring him any relief. He spent his money on doctors and shamans, but no one could figure out what was wrong with him let alone heal him. Then one day he thought about a god he had never prayed to before, the God of the Christians, named Jesus. He went into a larger neighboring town looking for someone who could tell him about that god. He could not find anyone, but he was able to locate a picture of Jesus in the market. He returned to his home and prayed to the picture of Jesus, asking to be healed. He fell asleep that night only to awaken the next morning completely healed. From that moment on, he told his family that he would no longer pray to any other gods, only to Jesus. As he shared this with us, he began to weep saying that he had waited many years to meet another follower of Jesus. He had thought perhaps he was the only one. That day a house fellowship was established with that man's family. And as we began to drive away from the village, an enormous rainstorm blew in and lasted for days, ending the drought as a sign of God's power.

Jesus said in John 3:3, "Very truly I tell you, no one can see the Kingdom of God unless they are born again." The blessing of Abraham to the nations is Christ Himself. He is the fulfillment of our hope. In Him we become new creations and enter into eternal relationship with His Father. The Bible says in Romans 6:23 that, "The wages of sin is death, but the gift of God is eternal life through Christ Jesus our Lord." Our sin stood as an impassable barrier keeping us from our promise of knowing God. The promise of Abraham stands before you today, Jesus Christ, the son of the living God. If you have never given your heart to Him, this is your day to begin a covenant with Christ. You are never too old or too young to receive this promise and as long as you are breathing, the promise of Christ is available to you.

After receiving this fire of revival, I desperately wanted to return to South Sudan and continue to work in the region where I had been serving in Upper Nile. During my time there, I had never seen any significant healing miracles (despite praying for hundreds of sick people). In other parts of South Sudan, I had seen incredible miracles, but it seemed that there was a tremendous block against the miracle ministry there in Upper Nile. Olivia and I along with a team from our church in Brownwood went and did several weeks of medical clinics along with showing *The Jesus Film*. Many people came to the Lord during this time, but still we saw no healing miracles.

A few months later I returned to Upper Nile. I felt strongly that I needed to go to a group of villages where our local friends had told me there were strongholds of witchcraft. Initially, the local Christians did not want to send me or go with me but after some convincing they sent me off with a few of the young men and elders from the church. We climbed into a wooden dugout canoe and went across the Sobat river, a large African river that flows out of Ethiopia. When we got to the other side, we began a two-week hike through the grasslands and swamps to visit the villages in the area. We all carried spears and machetes to protect ourselves from the lions and wild animals in the bush.

One day as we were hiking through a swampy area near the river, I heard the voice of the enemy say that I had stepped into his territory and that he would kill me. This voice came out of nowhere and shook me; I looked around to see if anyone else had heard it. I was surprised no one else had. I began thinking about all the ways to die there in the bush of South Sudan. It suffices to say there are many ways to die there. My mind immediately went to what I should do to prevent my death: Should I go back? Turn around? Leave South Sudan? I knew none of those were truly an option. I could not shake the thought that I had finally found a wife but would die in the bush before ever having the chance to get married! Suddenly, in that moment the Lord brought to my mind a Scripture I had memorized many times but never really understood: Romans 8. After getting out of the swamp, I opened my Bible and began to read this Scripture and saw something I had never seen before.

> Likewise, the Spirit helps us in our weakness. For we do not know what to pray for as we ought, but the Spirit himself intercedes for us with groanings too deep for words. And he who searches hearts knows what is the mind of the Spirit, because the Spirit intercedes for the saints according to the will of God. And we know that for those who love God all things work together for good, for those who are called according to his purpose.
>
> Romans 8:26-28

Like many Christians I had memorized those comforting words, "And we know that for those who love God all things work together for good, for those who are called according to his purpose." However, I had never seen it in this context of warfare in the Spirit. I began to pray in tongues and for the next few weeks I prayed almost constantly in the Spirit. I began to pray not out of a fearful mentality but as someone who had a covenant with my God! Day and night as I prayed, I felt a supernatural peace.

One night as we were showing *The Jesus Film* in a local village, I was sitting with some of my traveling companions preparing food and filtering water that we had taken from the river. It was a very dark night. I sat there listening to the sounds of the movie that echoed through the night air outside the hut. I got up from the small cooking fire and reached out my hand to get my portable water filter that I had hanging from the grass thatch roof inside the dark hut.

Suddenly one of the elders jumped up, grabbed my hand and pulled me back. He reached down to grab a machete and swung it into the dark space above the water filter. A black mamba snake fell down to the floor and was promptly killed by our team. The black mamba is one of Africa's most venomous snakes—they call it the two-step snake because once it bites a person, they usually only take about two steps before they fall down dead. I looked at the snake dumbfounded. How could this man have seen a dark black snake in a grass roof where there was no electricity or lights? It was truly a miracle. Standing there looking down at the body of this deadly serpent I was reminded of the enemy's voice I had heard a few weeks before and God's miraculous protection for me that night. We as believers are not defenseless in the face of our adversary. The Bible says that the Spirit helps us when we do not know what to pray. When we pray in tongues, the Spirit intercedes and begins to change the reality of our circumstances to align us with the perfect will of God.

God has a plan for our lives, but in the middle of the battle we must learn to claim and walk in the covenant that we have already received. The Bible says that satan prowls about like a roaring lion, seeking who he may devour. God desires to firmly establish us in our covenant and empower us with His Spirit so that the enemy cannot take us out before our time.

After the encounter with the snake and hearing the voice of the devil, I felt more than ever that God wanted to do miracles among the people in these villages so that their faith would truly be based upon the power of God. However, despite praying for many sick people, I didn't see anyone healed. In other parts of Africa and within South Sudan where I had traveled, I saw God do many miracles resulting in people being truly born again. But in this region of Upper Nile, I had never seen a physical healing.

A few days after the snake incident, I returned to the main village where I was based. I decided to host a gathering of pastors and leaders from other denominations. I simply told them what the tribal elders had told me years before, and asked if any of them had seen God do miracles in this region. They all began to recount stories of the revivals where they had received the Lord in the refugee camps in Kenya, Uganda and northern Sudan. I asked again, "has anyone of you seen God do miracles here?" They all replied no, and some began to comment that it was because of the spiritual strongholds or principalities in the region or because of the lack of faith in the people. After all the pastors had spoken, the Lord gave me a word saying that it was not the faith of the unbelievers or the strongholds of the demonic spirits, but it was the doubt and unbelief in the churches that was the problem. The Holy Spirit fell and we began to repent. Many people fell on the ground and wept before the Lord repenting for our doubt and unbelief. Some of them were baptized in the Holy Spirit and began to speak in tongues for the first time. After hours of prayer like this, we knew that something had shifted in our hearts.

Olivia and Karin Ashcraft conducting medical clinics in Upper Nile state.

Banjara women in their colorful local clothes.

Crossing the Sobat river in a canoe.

We walked long distances through these swamps to visit villages inaccessible by any kind of road.

Fellowshipping with the local congregation in Baliet, Upper Nile.

CHAPTER 7

THE FULFILLMENT

A few days after experiencing this small taste of revival, we set out again for evangelism in the remote villages across the river. We spent several weeks hiking and showing *The Jesus Film*. We continued to preach the gospel and pray for the sick, but nothing happened as we prayed. There were still no healings or miracles. One day, however, when we arrived to a new village, I decided to go out house-to-house to pray for people and preach the gospel. We arrived at one house and saw a very old blind lady sitting by the door. She and her daughter lived together and they were both widows. They lived in unimaginable poverty. We asked her if we could pray for her, and I laid my hands on her eyes and began to pray. I was very tired and sick from malaria and frustrated because of all the times I had prayed for people and not seen them healed. As I prayed for her, a very honest prayer came out of my mouth in English. "God, if you don't show up, I quit! If you are not here, I don't want to continue like this anymore. I cannot do it anymore!" As I stood there, lost in my prayers of doubt, the women reached out her hand and tugged on my shirt saying in Dinka, "I see you, I see you!"

"You see me?" I asked.

"Yes," she replied and then began to describe to us everything she could now see perfectly. Her daughter wept seeing her mother's eyesight restored and we led them both to Christ. After the word of these miracles had spread, people began to come out to our meetings in groups of thousands. Many received the Lord during this time. I was approached by some of the same elders who had mocked the gospel when I had arrived years before. These men said that they now believed in Jesus and wanted to be baptized in His name!

In 2013 Olivia and I were married. I could not believe that God had blessed me in such a way. I was also offered an opportunity to study for my master's in business administration. We continued to go back and forth to Africa and Mexico during that time and saw God do many miracles. It was a fulfillment to what God had promised years ago that He would bring my wife to me and that together we would fulfill the call of God on our lives.

> ...the God of Isaac...
>
> Exodus 3:6, NIV

With these words God reminded Moses that although his people seemed forgotten and abandoned in Egypt, God would never forget the promises He made. He is the God who fulfills His word. Isaac represented the fulfillment of a promise to Abraham. Abraham chose to name him Isaac, which means "laughter or joy." Because of this fulfilled promise, joy returned to Abraham's house. Isaac also followed in Abraham's footsteps in his walk of faith. God continually reminded him of the covenant He had made with his father. But after Abraham died, the Philistines began to come against Isaac. They quarreled with him, forced him out, and stopped up his wells.

> Isaac reopened the wells that had been dug in the time of his father Abraham, which the Philistines had stopped up after

Abraham died, and he gave them the same names his father had given them.

Genesis 26:18, NIV

Having a promise from God is wonderful, but walking it out can be the hard part. Have you ever noticed that shortly after God gives you a word, the warfare becomes more intense than ever? The reason the enemy does this is because he wants to convince us to let go of our promise, give up, and conform to his reality. The Philistines both feared and envied Abraham and Isaac. They envied their prosperity and wanted them to fail. They feared their growing numbers, for that reason they stopped up their wells. In the desert, water is everything. Having a good well represents the difference between life and death for a village. In ancient times, invading armies would often poison or fill in the wells in places where they invaded in order to thoroughly defeat their enemies. Whoever controlled the water, had the power. The goal of the Philistines was to either drive out Isaac or bring him under submission to their will. Either compromise would have required Isaac to give up his promised land. Isaac however, would not be driven out. So instead of giving up, he and his family picked up their tools and began to re-dig the wells of promise. In much the same way the devil comes into our lives with one purpose in mind:

> The thief comes only to steal and kill and destroy; I came that they may have life and have it abundantly.
>
> John 10:10

The devil comes to steal our promise from the Father. He cannot, however, simply take it away. We must choose to give it up. There are serious restrictions to his ability to harm us based on our covenant with God. Abraham and Isaac's lives were prophetic. In the same way that Isaac opened up the wells that his father had dug, Jesus comes into our lives and restores unto us the well of life which flows from our relationship with the Father. Our enemy is constantly trying to plug up our well of promise.

Once while ministering in a church in Mexico, a young woman came to my wife and I to receive prayer. She was a part of a very conservative Pentecostal church that loved God but, in many ways, seemed stuck in the 1950's. Everyone dressed a certain way, and in every service, there was a lot of crying and very little joy. As we were praying for her, she began to confess a horrible abuse that had happened to her many years ago that she had never told to anyone outside her family. She had been abused by a family member who was part of the church. When she tried to talk to her parents (who were pastors), they told her to never speak about it again. She felt dirty, unloved and unheard. For many years she had been disillusioned, running from God and not trusting the church. When she came back to the Lord, she wanted to connect with Him through prayer and crying but she could not get delivered from the hatred she carried inside. As she confessed this to us, we led her in a simple prayer to forgive her abuser. She hung her head and wept, as she had done many times before. My wife and I lifted her head and looked her in the eyes and said, "That's enough tears. God wants to restore your joy in Him." Suddenly, she began to laugh uncontrollably as God healed her from many years of trauma. She laid on the ground filled with such joy that tears streamed down her face. After a few minutes, she got up and said "I need to take this to my church." She took off running into the sanctuary laughing and weeping. The people were shocked but many began to be touched by the same joy that had fallen on her and began falling over laughing under the power of God. This joy completely healed her from years of pain and gave her the ability to love the church where she had been so hurt in the past.

The Lord desires to restore our joy in Him. Joy is far more than simply laughter Joy is something that flows out of the well of our relationship with Christ. It is part of the fruit of the Holy Spirit and is essential for the believer. Perhaps in your life you feel that the enemy has stopped up the well of God's presence and you need to be reconnected to this flow of the Holy Spirit! Jesus spoke of our great need to drink from the river of the Holy Spirit:

> On the last and greatest day of the festival, Jesus stood and said in a loud voice, "Let anyone who is thirsty come to me and

drink. Whoever believes in me, as Scripture has said, rivers of living water will flow from within them".

John 7:37-38, NIV

You and I each have a desperate need to have this river of God flowing in us. If you have Jesus, you have access to the Holy Spirit's river. He wants to baptize you into this river and allow it to then overflow out of you.

Once our ministry took a team from a church in Iowa on a mission trip to Reynosa. During a church service, the team was praying for people to be baptized in the Holy Spirit. One older woman came to the front, saying she had always wanted to speak in tongues. A young lady on the team named Diana prayed for her. Diana did not speak any Spanish and the woman could not speak English, but as the Holy Spirit fell on the woman, Diana was shocked to hear the woman prophesying in perfect English. Later on through an interpreter, Diana asked the woman if she had understood what she had said. The women replied that she did not understand it. Diana then went on to explain the prophecy that the woman had spoken in English. Both were completely overwhelmed by the goodness of God. God desires that the power of the Holy Spirit should flow out of every believer. If the river is flowing out of us, there should be constant fruit of this powerful river. Once I was speaking at a school of ministry with students from many countries around the world. After a short time of worship, I was given the mic to begin teaching. I felt in my spirit that the Lord wanted to do some things. I began to pray in tongues and invited everyone to continue worshipping the Lord. Suddenly, a girl began to shout and dance. I didn't think anything of it and continued singing out loud in tongues until another girl came running up to the front weeping and fell to the floor. I prayed for her and continued with my sermon while she laid on the ground and wept. She was down for several hours. After finishing my lesson both girls approached me, the one who had been dancing asked where I had learned to speak Hebrew. I replied that I had never studied Hebrew and cannot speak it. The first girl replied that she was a Palestinian from Israel and that she spoke fluent Hebrew. She said when I was speaking in tongues she understood every word I was saying, and that I had been prophesying about Jesus! She began to scream because God was doing a powerful work in her heart to forgive and love her Jewish neighbors. The fact that God would give her a word in Hebrew meant so much to her.

The other girl then began to share her story with me. She told me how she had been raised in a very religious orthodox home but had an encounter with Jesus a number of years ago. Her family was furious and tried everything they could to get her to reject her newfound faith in Jesus. For her safety she was forced to flee and change her name. She remained very traumatized from the experience. During the worship, she was sitting in the back of the room telling God that she was ready to quit because she felt so alone. Everything in her life was just too painful. Then suddenly, she heard me call her out by her name in Hebrew, not in her current name, but her given name that she had changed years before. The Holy Spirit spoke to her through me, speaking to her personally by name saying that her heavenly Father was calling her. Three times this phrase rang out. She sat there dumbfounded for a moment until she grasped the reality that God Himself was speaking to her! She jumped up screaming and ran into the embrace of her heavenly Father, where she encountered healing in His arms! The baptism of the Holy Spirit is really a baptism into the love and power of our heavenly Father. It empowers us to flow with His Spirit and better reveal the nature of our Father to those around us in a supernatural way.

If you have never received the baptism of the Holy Spirit, the Lord desires to open a well within you. It is easy to receive the Holy Spirit, you simply need to say yes to Him. Jesus said,

> And I tell you, ask, and it will be given to you; seek, and you will find; knock, and it will be opened to you. For everyone who asks receives, and the one who seeks finds, and to the one who knocks it will be opened.
>
> Luke 11:9-10

Just like the lady who heard God speaking to her in her heart language, calling her out by her name, God is calling you today.

Many believers are afraid of the supernatural gift of tongues simply because they do not understand. I have had people ask me,

"How can I know I am truly receiving the Holy Spirit and not an evil spirit?"

Or "How can I know for sure that I am receiving a legitimate gift of tongues and not simply making noises?"

These are valid questions that Jesus very clearly answered for us in the gospel of Luke.

> What father among you, if his son asks for a fish, will instead of a fish give him a serpent; or if he asks for an egg, will give him a scorpion? If you then, who are evil, know how to give good gifts to your children, how much more will the heavenly Father give the Holy Spirit to those who ask him!
>
> Luke 11:11-13

In this passage, Jesus gives us the keys to receiving the true Holy Spirit.

1. First, we must be born again. The Holy Spirit is for those who have trusted Jesus as their savior. It does not matter how long you have been a Christian, whether it be 5 minutes or 50 years. Any true follower of Jesus can receive the gift of the Holy Spirit.

2. Ask God in prayer to give you the Holy Spirit and baptize you in His fiery presence.

3. Trust that your heavenly Father will give you this gift.

4. Open your mouth and begin to speak in new tongues. It may sound strange to you at first to speak in a language that you do not understand, but as you pray you will feel His power and His presence flowing in your life.

5. After receiving this gift, begin to use it every day in prayer and worship. You can speak in tongues; you can also sing in tongues! This gift helps us grow closer in our relationship with the Lord!

When the heads of families and tribal leaders began to decide to follow Jesus, it opened the way for many of their wives and children to follow after them.

We saw many of these precious people decide to follow Jesus during this time.

Baptizing local village elders in the Sobat River.

On the shores of Lake Victoria, in Uganda, where I asked Olivia to marry me.

Traveling and preaching the gospel in remote villages in Africa.

CHAPTER 8

THE NEW BEGINNING

I have always been drawn to places of conflict, not because I am an adrenaline junkie or derive any joy from dangerous situations. But because I love to see God transform the most unlikely people and places for His glory! It was this passion to see the power of God break out in violent places that led us to Tamaulipas, Mexico. While Olivia and I were living and studying in the USA, I began to read newspaper articles of the incredible violence that had engulfed the cities of Reynosa and Nuevo Laredo. In these articles I saw horrific images of mass graves, decapitated bodies and the carnage of gun battles. Something touched my heart and compelled me to go.

Kelly Crenshaw, my friend and pastor from Brownwood, and I decided to take a prayer trip to visit every border city from Laredo to the Gulf of Mexico. We set off in my little Saturn car, arriving in Laredo, Texas. We crossed the border into Nuevo Laredo and met with a small group of pastors there. While praying together, we heard what sounded like rain pouring down on the roof. This seemed very odd since it was a sunny day. I got up off my knees and looked outside. It was clear and sunny without a cloud in the sky. I was perplexed because I could still hear the rain. I looked around the room and other pastors were looking out the windows confused as well. Almost everyone could hear the sound of rain. We marveled at this sign and wonder. The next town we went to was called Ciudad Guerrero; it had been on the news because a missionary couple had been shot off their jet ski by the cartel on the lake that sits on the border. The Mexican military had also found a number of mass graves of people that had been killed during the violence. As we approached the city, the Mexican military stopped us and asked our reason for coming. We explained that we were there to pray. They all looked at us quizzically and said, "You need to go back, it's too dangerous here." We persisted that we were determined to go. One of the soldiers began to laugh and said, "You're crazy, but if you want to die, go ahead and go. We'll just say goodbye now because we won't see you again alive." They let us go and with those comforting words ringing in our ears we drove into Ciudad Guerrero.

We found a local church and knocked on the door of the parsonage. The pastor saw us, and looked very surprised. He explained that he had not seen white missionaries there in years. We told him that our mission was to come and pray for these cities and pour out oil. He introduced us to another pastor. Both of them shared about the horrific things that had happened there over the past few years. Many people had fled the town and those that remained did not want to leave their houses except for work. Their church numbers had shrunk and they felt totally defeated. We went to the lake and began to pray. As we poured out olive oil on the ground, a huge gust of wind blew out of nowhere. We all looked around amazed at this wind that had suddenly started blowing on such a calm day. We left Ciudad Guerrero later that evening, making sure to say hello to the soldiers so they could see that we were still alive.

...and the God of Jacob...

Exodus 3:6, NIV

In the culture of the Old Testament, a name was more than just something to be known by. It spoke into a person's nature. Sometimes the meanings of names were powerful and prophetic, other times names carried a dark meaning. The name Jacob literally means "heel grabber, supplanter or trickster." This was Jacob's nature, he was a conniver who tricked those around him into getting what he wanted. He tricked his brother into giving up his birthright, and he tricked his father into giving him the blessing of the firstborn. He seemed to be able to out connive everyone around him until he met his uncle Laban. He was tricked into years of servitude to his uncle. Finally after years of living in a foreign land, he left with his family to return to the country that was his birthright—but there was a problem. In order to receive his inheritance, he had to face the mistakes of his past. He had to meet with his brother Esau who he had defrauded, his brother who he was sure would want him dead. However, while he was on his way there, he had an encounter with God in the wilderness that would forever change his name, his heart and his walk.

> So Jacob was left alone, and a man wrestled with him till daybreak. When the man saw that he could not overpower him, he touched the socket of Jacob's hip so that his hip was wrenched as he wrestled with the man. Then the man said, "Let me go, for it is daybreak."
>
> But Jacob replied, "I will not let you go unless you bless me."
>
> The man asked him, "What is your name?"
>
> "Jacob," he answered.
>
> Then the man said, "Your name will no longer be Jacob, but Israel, because you have struggled with God and with humans and have overcome."
>
> Jacob said, "Please tell me your name."
>
> But he replied, "Why do you ask my name?" Then he blessed him there. So Jacob called the place Peniel, saying, "It is because I saw God face to face, and yet my life was spared."
>
> Genesis 32:24-30, NIV

If we submit to God's process, the grace of God can thoroughly change everything about us and give us a new beginning. Once God had Jacob alone, He wrestled with him. Jacob had spent his entire life up until that point wrestling against God and man.

Once while I was ministering in a neighborhood in Reynosa, Mexico, I came to the small house of a couple I had prayed with before. They were believers and invited me into their house and introduced me to their son. He shook my hand but was being very evasive. He tried to leave but since I was standing in the doorway he could not easily escape. I asked if I could pray for him. He told me not now, because he had something he had to do. The Lord gave me a word that he had pain in his ribs so I asked him if he was in pain. "Yes," he answered, surprised. I replied that Jesus wanted to heal him. He finally said yes, that I could pray for a few minutes, but that he really needed to go afterwards. I laid hands on his shoulders and began to pray. I watched as a look of surprise came across his face. He began to weep as all the pain left his body. He moved his arms and legs and exclaimed with a shocked look that he had no more pain. I invited him to our house church meeting that we would be having in a few minutes. He again tried to convince me he was busy but finally dropped the excuse and said he would go to church with me. A few minutes later he was sitting in the worship service with us, tears streaming down his face. After the message he stood up and announced that he wanted to give his heart to Jesus. He began to cry as he told us his story. He had been part of a local gang and a week or so before he had gotten in a fight with some rivals. They cracked his ribs and beat him severely so he was at his parents' house recovering. The day I arrived was going to be his first day to leave the house and he was on his way to kill the people who had done this to him. All he could think about was revenge, until Jesus encountered him and healed his body. He repented and forgave his enemies and gave his life to Jesus!

There is something in each of us like Jacob that fights against the working of the Holy Spirit in us. We must come face-to-face with the utter futility of our struggle against the Almighty in order to find a place of complete surrender. But what was it that kept God from killing Jacob that day? Jacob was a liar; he was stubborn and disobedient, but despite his past he desperately wanted the blessing of God. He knew full well that he could have easily died from his encounter, but something inside of him compelled him to not let go of the Lord. This is the kind of stubborn faith that pleases God. In the Old Testament people knew that if you saw God's face you would die. Yet to those saints who persisted in God's presence, such as Abraham, Enoch, Jacob (and eventually Moses himself), God broke His own rules and allowed them to see Him and speak to Him face-to-face. But these encounters were costly, they did not know if they would survive. Yet the pursuit of the presence was of greater value to these men than their own lives. This is the kind of hunger that pleases God. This is the kind of reckless abandon that causes a man or woman to step into a place of encounter that forever changes the way they walk with Him. In that place of encounter, God changed Jacob's name to Israel. The name Israel means "who wrestles with God and prevails." The connotation in Hebrew is that Israel was one who would stubbornly cling to God and would not let go. Jacob's name was changed by a word from God. His identity, however, was changed by the encounter. I believe that God mentioned the name Jacob to Moses at the burning bush because He desired for Moses to know that He was the only one capable of forgiving his murderous past and giving him a new beginning.

As Kelly and I continued our trip along the border, we stopped and prayed in several other towns that day. We were stopped on various occasions by the cartel and the military, but God continued to give us favor. We stopped in a city called Reynosa. We had the contact of an American pastor who worked there. He met us and took us through the city. We went to a little park near the border and began to pray. We poured out oil on the ground as a prophetic symbol of God's anointing and began to pray for His presence to be poured out there in that city. As we prayed, the Lord gave me a prophetic word to release over the city.

I began to prophesy that the Lord was sending a great awakening to Mexico that would impact the nations and that out of that revival would come a missionary sending movement; that the Lord desired to raise up a school of missions. People would come from the north, south, east and west to be trained in Reynosa and sent out.

Everyone was excited about what God would do! I left Reynosa, excited that we had played a small part in what God desired to do although I firmly believed that I would not be there to see it because I would be moving to Africa.

About a year later, Olivia and I were leading a missions team to Morelos state located in the southern part of Mexico. We spent several weeks ministering in many different churches. Toward the end of the trip, we were invited to minister at a youth conference in a town called Jojutla. We weren't the primary speakers but they invited us up to minister towards the end of worship. There was an incredible anointing of God filling the room to the point where many young people began to fall down on the floor and worship Jesus. I was about to speak when my wife walked up and asked me for the mic. Olivia is typically very quiet and does not like to speak much publicly, so when she comes to speak, I know she has heard the Lord. She took the mic and began to release a prophetic word.

She began to prophesy that the Lord was longing for His Mexican bride, and that He was about to bring revival into this nation. The revival that would be coming to Mexico would be a revival unlike anything ever seen before. This coming revival would be unique to Mexico and it would come out of the younger generation. It would be a revival written in the history books. It would be a strong outpouring of the Holy Spirit that would sweep north, south, east and west.

People were powerfully touched during the ministry time; many were falling to the floor weeping and crying out for this outpouring. After the service had finished, we went into the foyer where a young man in the audience approached us. He asked Olivia, "Do you believe what you said?"

"Of course," she replied. "If I did not believe it, I would not have said it."

Again, he asked, "Do you believe what you said?"

She walked away from that conversation somewhat confused. Why did he ask the question twice? We returned back to Texas while I finished up my MBA, and we continued with our plans to move to Africa. We thought we knew God's will but found out we were in for a surprise.

While we were living in Brownwood, I would go most mornings to pray at a Christian coffee shop on campus. One morning as I was praying, I heard the Lord speak very clearly to me.

He asked me a question, "Do you remember what you prophesied in Reynosa?"

"Yes!" I replied. "Revival, school of missions, and missionaries going into the world!"

"Yes," He replied, "but that word was not for the people you spoke it to, that word is for you. Now move to Reynosa and do what I have told you to do."

On one of our first ministry trips to Morelos, Mexico. Preaching with Arturo Higuera, cofounder of Kaleo in that country.

We saw so many powerful miracles during these simple tent meetings!

CHAPTER 9

FACE-TO-FACE WITH GOD

I sat there stunned in silence. For many years I had planned to serve in Africa. I had never dreamed that I would ever live long term in Latin America. I wanted to be on the cutting edge of pioneer missions and go to the darkest war zones to plant churches among unreached people groups. Now I was being told to go to a city where there were plenty of churches, to live only miles away from the United States. My heart was broken but I said yes to the Lord. I thought to myself, how will I tell my wife about this huge change of plans?

I returned to my house and told my wife that we needed to talk because God had spoken to me about what His next steps for us were. I went with her to a local coffee shop and told her what the Lord had spoken to me. She began to cry, and told me what God had spoken to her. After her prophetic word in Jojutla, she asked the Lord why the young man came and asked her twice if she believed the word or not. It seemed to be a strange question to ask. As she prayed the Lord spoke clearly to her and said that the first time he asked it was him, but the second time he asked it was a question from the Lord. If she believed in that word, was she willing to move to Mexico to help see this revival birthed. She replied that she was willing, but God would have to make it clear to me. For several weeks she quietly guarded this word in her heart and waited for the Lord to confirm it through me. We both sat in silent awe at this tremendous change of plans. As we prayed, we both trembled with a holy fear of the Lord as we recognized the magnitude of this new plan..

> At this, Moses hid his face, because he was afraid to look at God.
>
> Exodus 3:6, NIV

The holiness of God is not something to be taken lightly. C.S. Lewis in his famous book *The Chronicles of Narnia* described the lion representing Jesus in this way, "He is not safe, but He is good." Encountering an almighty God is meant to shake us down to our very core. When Moses encountered this all-powerful Being in the fire, he hid his face. Although Moses did not fully understand it, he was being trained in the fire for his assignment to lead the people of Israel. God was also testing him, because before he could be trusted with the anointing to break the idolatrous power of Pharaoh and lead the people out of slavery, the Lord needed to see that Moses feared Him. As the Proverbs say,

> The fear of the Lord is the beginning of wisdom, and knowledge of the Holy One is understanding.
>
> Proverbs 9:10, NIV

The fear of the Lord is not the same as simply being afraid of God. The fear of the Lord calls us closer. It is a holy fear that leads us to take steps of radical obedience. God's love language is obedience and an encounter with God is meant to change in us what needs to be changed so that we will obey his call with our whole heart. God is more interested in the journey with you than you simply fulfilling a task. On the journey we learn to follow and trust Him. On the journey we learn obedience to His voice and call.

We immediately began making plans to move to Reynosa. Our friends and family were truly surprised that we would take such a radical turn. One week before we were scheduled to leave, we received a letter in the mail from our biggest donor. This organization represented almost 90% of our monthly support. These dear friends had known me since I was 9 years old and had supported me since the beginning of my ministry. They had always followed my journey with the Holy Spirit and had respected my experiences with the Holy Spirit even though it was different than their particular church. However, they had just read a book by John McArthur talking about how Charismatics were heretics, and that the gifts of the Holy Spirit were not needed in our modern day. For that reason, they felt they could no longer support our ministry unless we agreed to go to an approved seminary and break all ties with the charismatic movement. We both sat there reading this letter, stunned. This letter only served as confirmation for us that we were on the right track. We thanked our friend for their years of support but replied that we would not be going to the seminary they suggested but would be moving to Mexico. Shortly after, another one of our primary supporters passed away. Word was also starting to spread that we had become "too charismatic," which caused other churches who had helped us to distance themselves from us. By the time we left for Mexico, we had lost 95% of our monthly support. However, we knew that God was calling and we were determined to obey His voice.

When we moved into Reynosa, we moved into a city at war. The battles between the cartels had spun out of control to the point where the government sent in the military. This resulted in bloody street battles between multiple heavily armed factions. Convoys of armored combat vehicles would battle it out on the street often while helicopters fired from above. Oftentimes buses would be set on fire in the roads to block the army from pursuing the escaping cartel soldiers. Ambushes, kidnappings, murders and combat fatalities were everyday news in those days. We came into this environment thrilled at the opportunity to serve Jesus in this place. We did not have any money, but a friend who was a pastor owned a partially finished medical clinic where he invited us to live and plant a church together.

We jumped into this work with our whole hearts and began reaching out to our neighbors. People began to come to the Lord and the church began to grow; within just a few months the church had grown to around 50 people. We began to conduct outreaches at the garbage dumps where the poorest of the poor live and work. God did many miracles in those days: people were healed of cancer and other chronic sicknesses. We had very little but were so excited to serve the people around us. We lived in the back room of the medical clinic. We had no money for repairs so we hung curtains for doors and put a tin roof on the 2nd floor so that we could plant a church.

Many families work in the garbage dumps sorting through trash before it is burned and buried. It is backbreaking, dangerous work that destroys the health of the people who do it day in and day out.

We were able to provide food, clothes and help to many of the families who lived and worked in the dump.

The building where we planted our first church in Reynosa, Mexico.

As we ministered and discipled people in the garbage dump, we were thrilled to see many of the families finding better work in other areas. Many people were set free from demons and generational curses.

Installing the roof with Pastor Kelly Crenshaw and a team from Brownwood, TX.

CHAPTER 10

SETTING THE CAPTIVES FREE

While in Reynosa, we began to see God do incredible miracles among some of the poorest of the poor. One day our ministry team was going house-to-house doing evangelism in a squatter camp in Reynosa. The team came to the house of a man who had been hit by a bus and had been paralyzed ever since. They began to pray for him and tried to help him get out of bed. They sat him up and laid hands on his back and suddenly they felt bones begin to pop and realign in his back and hips. He stood up much to the surprise of his family and began to walk around. He grabbed his crutches and ran outside and threw them out into the street. He immediately turned to our team and said that he wanted to give his life to Christ and be baptized. We took the formerly paralyzed man down to the river bank and baptized him in the canal as a testimony to his community!

> The LORD said, "I have indeed seen the misery of my people in Egypt. I have heard them crying out because of their slave drivers, and I am concerned about their suffering".
>
> Exodus 3:7, NIV

I once had a man come up to me at a conference I was speaking at, asking for my mantle and anointing. I replied that I could not give him my mantle because that had to come from God. I would pray however for God to take him through the same process He had brought me through. I started praying, "Lord thank you for taking my brother to the darkest places of the world. I thank you that He will fear you above all else and that he will not love his life so much as to shrink from death." I guess this was not the prayer he was wanting or expecting because the man took off running and I never saw him again. Sometimes the danger for us as believers is that we want the fire without the sacrifice. We want the glory without the process and we want the mantle without the mandate. For Moses it was not enough to simply have an encounter, he had to also choose to accept the mission that was placed before him to see the captives set free.

We must never forget as Christians that God gives us the power of His Spirit for much more than just simply to bless us. He empowers us with His Spirit in order to partner with Him in seeing the captives set free! In much of the church, we have lost our vision of seeing captives set free and as a result we are not walking in the fullness of God's power. Where there is not vision for the lost there will not be many miracles. Jesus said,

> The Spirit of the Lord is upon me, because he has anointed me to proclaim good news to the poor. He has sent me to proclaim liberty to the captives and recovering of sight to the blind, to set at liberty those who are oppressed, to proclaim the year of the Lord's favor.
>
> Luke 4:18-19

Jesus fully recognized that the power of the Holy Spirit upon Him was for a purpose. In the Old Testament, priests, prophets and kings would be anointed with oil as a symbol of the Holy Spirit resting upon them. The anointing was meant to empower and set apart a person for a mission. Once my pastor Kelly Crenshaw was leading a team from our church on an outreach to Nuevo Laredo, Mexico. They felt they were supposed to go and pray on a bridge where one of the cartels had hung bodies with threats against the other cartels and the local government. Our team prayed on the bridge and while they were there they ministered to a man from the cartel who got saved. Our team had also been giving away Bibles and Christian books as they had done on many occasions in the local churches. A few nights later Pastor Kelly returned to Nuevo Laredo to preach at a church. After he spoke, he was approached by several women from one of the local churches asking for more of the oil that had been coming out of the books and Bibles our team had brought. Kelly was confused but through an interpreter the ladies explained that the Bibles had been leaking a fragrant oil and that they had been using it to anoint people for the past few days and that everyone who had been anointed was healed. This was amazing considering that none of our team had put any oil in the books. This was a supernatural manifestation of God's anointing on His Word!

The gospel truly is good news to the poor! Jesus said, "blessed are the poor in spirit." This phrase refers to more than economic poverty, it refers to people who recognize the great need they have for God. In my experience, the poor receive more from the Lord simply because they recognize how great their need is.

One night our team was doing a campaign in a community built near a garbage dump. The people in the community were very poor but very hungry for God. The women from the church had prepared food for the event but were surprised to find more people coming to the event than they had planned for. They prepared food for about 100 people but more and more people began to show up. They prayed over the food and continued to feed people. They had prepared 2 big pots but every time they dipped food out it just continued to multiply. In the end, we fed around 200 people as God continued to multiply the food. An elderly blind woman came into the meeting being led around by her grandson. After a botched cataract surgery, she had lost her vision in both eyes. Our team began to pray for her, she opened her eyes and began to weep as she realized she could see! She then began to describe what she saw around her as her family and community watched in amazement!

The Holy Spirit comes upon us to empower us to preach the gospel. We must learn as we preach to work with the Holy Spirit and ask Him constantly what he desires to do. When we do, He will often surprise us and touch people even when we are not expecting it. Once while visiting a small church in a small Ugandan town called Wobulenzie, we met with one of the local village leaders, an elderly man named Jamil. Don and Jackie Ragland had met him the previous year when they were ministering for a month in these villages. He was from another religion but had always been respectful to the Christians in his area. Don had shared the gospel with him before and although he was very open and allowed Don to pray for his home and family, he did not make a decision to receive Christ. This particular day as we gathered with a small group of people, we began to share the gospel and ask if anyone was in need of a healing. A number of people stood up to allow us to pray for them. At first Jamil just sat there as we began to pray for the sick. As God did miracles, people began to share what God had done. Jamil then stood up and came forward to receive prayer. Everyone quieted down as Jamil stood up. He had not told anyone there, but he had suffered a stroke which left one arm numb. He had lost his ability to grip with that hand. As we began to pray, he felt something like fire shoot into his hand and up his arm. After this happened, he realized that his hand and arm had been completely restored to full feeling and strength! He later publicly committed his life to Christ. Because of this miracle, about 5 or 6 others also gave their lives to Jesus. Jamil became a very open witness for the gospel and continued to travel around the villages preaching about the power of Jesus.

We have seen powerful miracles occur on many occasions as we worship Jesus. There is something incredibly powerful when anointed believers worship God in Spirit and truth! During a revival event in Reynosa, a man came running up to the front during the worship with his wife telling me excitedly that he could hear. I did not completely understand him because of the loud music. Later during the transition from worship into the preaching he began to tell me that he had been completely deaf for eleven years, but as he stood there with his wife during the worship service reading the lyrics on the screen, his ears suddenly opened and he heard worship for the first time in many years! He was completely overwhelmed with emotion and he and his wife came to the front because they could not wait and wanted to get saved right then and there.

When you read both the Old and New Testament there is one type of miracle that does not occur until Jesus comes upon the scene, and that is the miracle of deliverance from evil spirits. Many believers in developed countries do not believe in the supernatural realm. The faith of too many Christians is completely intellectual and does not leave room for the spiritual world around us. In most third world countries, however, there exists a strong realization of the spiritual world around them. People coming to Christ out of animistic backgrounds come with a completely different worldview.

After years of serving in these intense spiritual environments, I have come to the realization that you cannot have a truly successful ministry unless you learn to operate through the power of the Holy Spirit in your day-to-day life. During my season serving in South Sudan I had the opportunity to travel through many parts of the country training leaders, evangelizing and helping plant churches. In one village where we were ministering in the Eastern Equatorial state near the Ugandan border, we did a leadership seminar and open-air meetings for the church we were serving with. In rural communities where pastors and leaders have very little training and may not even be able to read the Bible, many traditional witchcraft practices can end up infiltrating the church.

We spent a weekend with a struggling church plant evangelizing and working with the leaders. One of the local leaders asked us if he was allowed to be an elder in the church since he had two wives. We explained that this was not Biblical for him to be a leader in the church. I along with an interpreter took him aside to minister to him. I asked him if he was born again. He replied that he was not because he had been told a man with two wives could not be saved. I told him that this was a lie, he could be saved but he should not become a church leader. He was very relieved to hear this. He then went on to tell me that for many years he had suffered from demonic spirits who came to him every night and caused him to convulse and have seizures. This started years ago when he went to the river and a demon spirit in the form of a frog jumped into him. His life was tormented ever since. I was a bit taken aback; this is not something they usually teach you how to deal with in the Western church! So, I told him we would start with him giving his life to the Lord, which he gladly did. I then laid hands on him and commanded the demons to leave. There was no manifestation, he just sat there quietly as I prayed. He told me that perhaps I would need to pray with him in the night when the demons usually tormented him.

All the men were camping out in an open field near the church. Some were sleeping in the back of a big covered flatbed truck. At 3 am I was awoken to the sounds of thrashing and screaming coming from the truck. I got up and went in the dark to the truck and found a man on his belly having a seizure. I prayed for him and commanded this spirit to leave. The man convulsed and then was set free from the demon. I rolled him over expecting to see the first man, only to discover that this was a different man. I told everyone to go back to sleep and that we would talk to him in the morning.

The next morning the first man I had prayed for came to me saying that during the night he heard the demons coming as he always had before and feared that they would torment him, but then he heard another voice, the voice of Jesus, saying, "This man is mine. Do not touch him!" After he heard this voice, the demons left and did not return. The second man who was from another village and did not know the first man then approached me, thanking me for casting the demon out of him. I asked him when this started and he gave me almost the exact same story about a demon in the form of a frog jumping into him years ago and causing him to have seizures ever since. This man also received Christ that day and was set free from years of demonic bondage. The seizures stopped from that day forward.

I know many Christians who are afraid of demons while others simply try to negate their existence. Yet when we look at the ministry of Jesus, we see that He constantly set people free from demonic bondage. In our world today there are many people who are quite literally prisoners to the demonic spirits that bind their minds and bodies.

One of the most powerful testimonies I have ever seen regarding deliverance occurred while a team from our ministry was visiting Honduras. While in a village, two missionaries with our organization encountered a young man named Santos who had quite literally been imprisoned because of demonic oppression.

Santos was born into a small village in the mountains of northern Honduras. He was a normal little 8-year-old boy with a loving family. One day, however, when he was walking through the jungle, he came across witchcraft items where a sacrifice had taken place. Being an innocent little child he picked up his new found "treasures" and returned to his home. His mother was horrified to see what he brought with him and yelled at him to return it to the jungle. Obediently, he ran back into the jungle to return the witchcraft items. No one knows what happened to Santos when he went back because he returned to his home completely changed. Whereas previously he had been a good student, he began to fail in school. He became increasingly violent over the next several months. He would disappear into the jungle for days at a time. Over the next two years, he lost the ability to talk and began simply grunting to communicate. By the time he was 10 years old, he had become so violent that his family had to take more drastic actions. His family, who were not Christians, had no idea what to do with him. In many developing countries there are no safety nets for people who are demonically oppressed or suffer from mental illness. The families will often have to improvise a solution to do the best they can.

Santos' family came to the decision as he grew bigger and more dangerous to tie him up to a post like an animal and lock him in a small room by himself. For 13 years, his mother would push plates of food to him with a stick to avoid being attacked and beaten. He would scream, and try to bite anyone who got too close. One day a team of Kaleo missionaries led by Don Ragland came to the village to do an outreach. People directed them to go and pray for Santos and his family. When they arrived, the family was very surprised that Don would want to pray for their son. He asked to go into the room, the family told him not to because Santos was violent and might attack him. They explained that in the past he had tried to bite, hit and even gouge out people's eyes who had gotten too close. But after talking with them for a while the family reluctantly agreed.

They unlocked the door to the dark little building and as Don entered in, he saw Santos completely naked except for a ragged, filthy old shirt, covered with his own feces and tied with ropes to a big post in the center of the room. His "tether" was only about one and a half meters long that had been the extent of Santos' world for the past 13 years. He had had no direct human contact for several years. He was extremely underweight. He had a wild animal kind of look in his eyes. He would crouch like a monkey and just grunt at you. Then he would urinate in the floor in front of you and laugh. Don and a local pastor began to pray in tongues and moved closer to the young man. They calmly cast the demonic spirits out of the man and went and sat next to him. His mother gasped, no one had gotten that close to her son without being attacked for 13 years. After an hour and a half, Santos stood up next to Don and laid his head on Don's shoulder and allowed Don to hug him. They laid hands on him and he was set free. The next day, his family saw so much improvement in his behavior that they cut off his ropes. He allowed them to clean him up and he started eating better. He gradually regained his speech and the ability to interact with other people. His entire family became Christians, and his brother began reading the Bible to Santos daily. Word spread fast in the community about the miracle that God had done. Even the local witch doctor was amazed at this deliverance and decided to renounce witchcraft and give her life to Jesus. A year later, Don and myself went back that village. We met with Santos who was a completely different man wearing clothes and walking free around his family farm. Jesus is the one who sets the captives free!

After being hit by a bus, this man could not walk without the use of crutches. He was in constant pain. After being healed, he gave his life to Christ and decided to be baptized!

Olivia giving food to one of the families who ran the horse cart trash service in Reynosa, México.

Most children who work in the garbage dump with their parents do not have the opportunity to go to school and become stuck in generational cycles of poverty. This photo was taken in Reynosa, Mexico.

Jamil, the village elder in Uganda dedicating his life publicly to Christ!

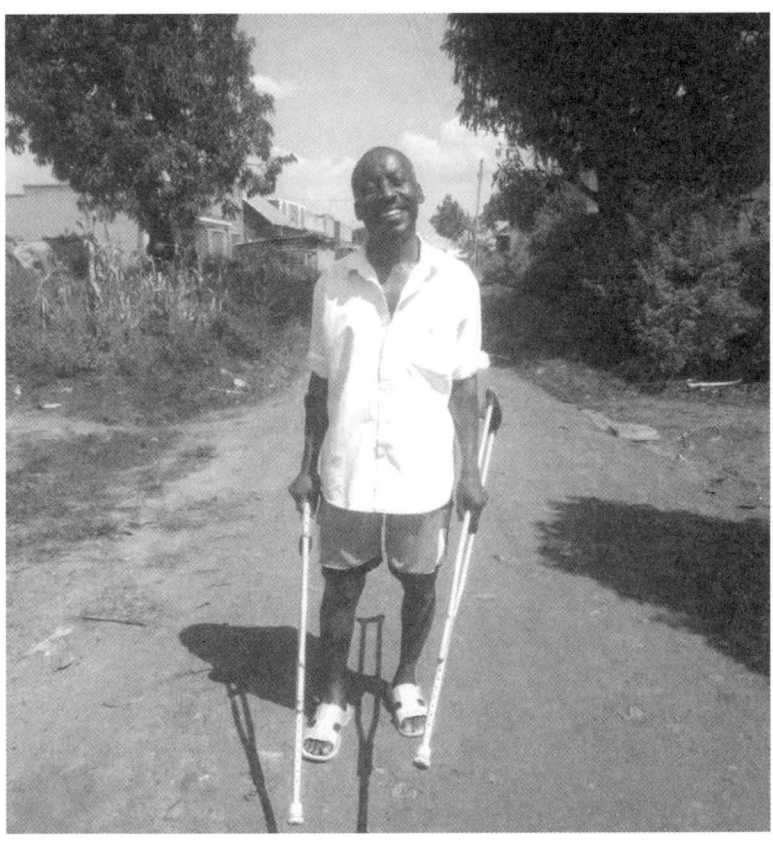

This man in Bwebajja, Uganda had been in a car wreck that broke his femur. The break never healed correctly and because of this he was in nearly constant pain. He could only walk short distances using crutches. We prayed for him at his house and he felt fire go into his body. Afterwards, he stood up and found that he could walk without any pain, later x-rays confirmed that the bone had been healed!

PART 3

SENT TO THE NATIONS

In the year that King Uzziah died, I saw the Lord, high and exalted, seated on a throne; and the train of his robe filled the temple. Above him were seraphim, each with six wings: With two wings they covered their faces, with two they covered their feet, and with two they were flying. And they were calling to one another:

"Holy, holy, holy is the LORD Almighty; the whole earth is full of his glory."

At the sound of their voices the doorposts and thresholds shook and the temple was filled with smoke.

"Woe to me!" I cried. "I am ruined! For I am a man of unclean lips, and I live among a people of unclean lips, and my eyes have seen the King, the LORD Almighty."

Then one of the seraphim flew to me with a live coal in his hand, which he had taken with tongs from the altar. With it he touched my mouth and said,

"See, this has touched your lips; your guilt is taken away and your sin atoned for."

Then I heard the voice of the Lord saying,

"Whom shall I send? And who will go for us?"

And I said,

"Here am I. Send me!"

He said,

"Go and tell this people: 'Be ever hearing, but never understanding; be ever seeing, but never perceiving'."

Isaiah 6:1-9, NIV

CHAPTER 11

WHO IS ON THE THRONE?

Before Olivia and I were married, we had both attended the Harvest School of Missions with Iris Ministries in Mozambique. God used this school to radically impact our lives, we encountered Him in a deep and powerful way while we were there. After we got married and God called us to Mexico, we felt that this was the model for the school we wanted to see birthed in Mexico that God had called us to plant. The Iris leadership invited us back to help staff one of the schools to be trained in how to start and lead a school of missions in Mexico. In 2014 while pioneering the work in Mexico, we went to staff the school in Mozambique. It was a powerful time and we learned so much. During that time we were honored to be officially ordained into ministry by Rolland and Heidi Baker and David Hogan. We firmly believe in impartation and this marked a powerful milestone in our lives and ministry.

> In the year that King Uzziah died, I saw the Lord, high and exalted, seated on a throne; and the train of his robe filled the temple.
>
> Isaiah 6:1, NIV

The book of Isaiah is full of prophesies about Jesus the Messiah. This short passage of Isaiah's call into ministry gives us a beautiful snapshot of what it means to be called by the Lord. Most scholars believe that Isaiah was from the line of King David and possibly a cousin to King Uzziah. Isaiah 6 records the life-changing encounter the prophet had with the Lord. In Isaiah's vision he saw the Lord lifted up above everything else. I think this illustrates a very important lesson for us today about the sovereignty of our King. Uzziah had been a good king who had ended badly. I am sure that Isaiah had been disappointed at the failure and subsequent death of this king. However, the vision of the Lord on the throne, changed everything for the prophet.

In our lives it can be easy to look at the little kings sitting on manmade thrones as having true power. I have seen Christians enter into absolute panic depending on how elections go in their country. I am not saying that Christians should disengage from politics, far from it, I am actually saying that our ministry to the kings of this world will be the most effective when we are consumed with the knowledge that an Eternal King sits above them on an everlasting throne. His rule will never be shaken by the circumstances around us. I have been to more than 50 nations and have personally seen that this gospel of Jesus Christ is powerful to save regardless of the type of government that is "in control." We are most effective when our eyes are firmly fixed on the one who sits on the throne. This puts everything else into focus and inspires a holy fear of the Lord in our hearts that the Bible says is the beginning of wisdom. This encounter with the Lord inspired a holy fear of the Lord in Isaiah's heart and prepared him to say yes to the commission.

For the believer, the fear of the Lord is far more than a fear of being punished by God. It is a holy awe because of the might and power of our Lord, birthed out of our great need for Him and based on the strong revelation that we cannot ever afford to live without Him. Many times, we talk about Jesus as our best friend. This is true. However, we can never forget that before He was our friend, He was the God who created everything that exists. He is the one who formed us and also the one who can destroy us. He is our friend, but he is first our King. This revelation of faith in Jesus as Lord and as God is the basis for truly being born again.

While in Mozambique, God showed me one of the most powerful examples I had ever experienced of His sovereign right to change our plans. One weekend we went to a village in the bush to show *The Jesus Film* and preach the gospel. We arrived in the remote village and began working to set up the generator and projector to show the movie. Despite our best efforts, the generator would not start. We also realized that two tires on one of the big trucks were flat. The entire team gathered around the machine to pray; many were rebuking demons, while others were asking God for a miracle. As I prayed, I heard the voice of the Lord say to me clearly.

"This is not a demon, this is my will."

I was thoroughly confused. I asked the Lord what I should do.

"Go tomorrow and fix the generator and the tires," came the reply.

The next morning, I went with a driver to a slightly larger neighboring village. We arrived and found a shop to fix the generator and went elsewhere to repair the tires. While we were sitting under a tree watching the men repair the tire, a man walked up to me asking me a question in the Makua language. I did not speak Makua so he switched to Portuguese (the official language of Mozambique). My Portuguese is limited so he then began to talk in Spanish. He explained that he had studied in Cuba many years ago. I was amazed to find someone in the middle of nowhere who spoke Spanish so we struck up a conversation. He then asked me if I would give him cigarettes. I laughed and replied no, that those things would kill him but I could give him something that would bring life to him. He looked at me puzzled, and then I shared the gospel with him. He was amazed to hear about the life of Jesus as he had never heard this message before. After a while of sharing, he said he wanted to follow

Christ. I led him in a simple prayer to receive Jesus. He then took me back to his home because he wanted his family to hear the gospel. He gathered his family together and interpreted into Makua for me as I shared the gospel. His mother, who was over 80 years old, sat there with tears in her eyes as I shared about Jesus.

She said, "I have lived for 80 years, through wars and famines but I have never heard this message of Jesus. Now I can die in peace because I know Jesus!" The entire family committed to follow Jesus together. As I was leaving, the man pointed to a lot next to his house and said, "I want to give this land to the Lord to build a church for Jesus." A few days later, I returned with the team to help establish a new church in the village. In much the same way as this woman, perhaps you have felt forgotten by God, waiting for many years for the fulfillment of a promise. Today is the day to give your life to Him.

The key to a successful prayer life is to find out what God is doing and begin to pray along those lines. Sometimes we do not pray according to His will because we have not come close enough to hear what His will is in the situation. Many believers struggle with obeying Jesus because they only understand Him as their friend but have not truly encountered Him as their king. Once you know Him first as king, it makes it much easier to obey Him even when His plans do not make sense.

> And after six days Jesus took with him Peter and James, and John his brother, and led them up a high mountain by themselves. And he was transfigured before them, and his face shone like the sun, and his clothes became white as light. And behold, there appeared to them Moses and Elijah, talking with him. And Peter said to Jesus, "Lord, it is good that we are here. If you wish, I will make three tents here, one for you and one for Moses and one for Elijah." He was still speaking when, behold, a bright cloud overshadowed them, and a voice from the cloud said, "This is my beloved Son, with whom I am well pleased; listen to him." When the disciples heard this, they fell on their faces and were terrified.
>
> Matthew 17:1-6

Who is on the Throne?

Peter, James and John were the inner circle of Jesus' disciples. These were the men who were invited into important intimate moments of Jesus' life and ministry that others did not see. In this story, they saw their friend meeting with Elijah and Moses. Jesus' face was shining with glory and was transfigured before their eyes. Peter had what seemed to him like a good idea in the moment to build tabernacles for Jesus, Moses and Elijah. He realized that his friend was an important prophet, speaking to the most important prophetic leaders of Jewish history. He saw his opportunity to curry favor with the prophets by helping Jesus build a shrine to these three men. As soon as he spoke, he was corrected by God the Father. The booming voice of the King would shake the disciples to their core and serve as an everlasting reminder to Peter that his friend was more than a prophet, and more than an earthly king; he was the everlasting God!

For followers of Jesus there is a fine line to walk between Jesus my savior and friend and Jesus the all-powerful king. Is He our friend or is He our king? The answer to that is yes, He is eternally both. Jesus truly desires to invite us into a deep friendship with Himself. We were created for intimacy and fellowship with God. However, friendship takes time to forge. Jesus called His disciples saying to follow Him, and He taught them how to serve, but before He was crucified, He no longer looked at them as servants but truly as his friends.

> No longer do I call you servants, for the servant does not know what his master is doing; but I have called you friends, for all that I have heard from my Father I have made known to you.
>
> John 15:15

This passage talks of the beauty of friendship with God; the fact that He would choose to invite us into His presence as His friends to be part of the fulfillment of His plan on the earth. It is a beautiful invitation to be friends of Jesus, but we can never forget that He is first our king.

Ministry is challenging and can be extremely messy but understanding the sovereignty of God strengthens us when circumstances seem to be completely in contrary to the words of promise we have received from the Lord. When we left Mexico to go to Mozambique for the summer, everything seemed to be going well. We did not realize that the pastor we were working with there was becoming jealous of our ministry. Olivia and I believed that this season in Reynosa would be just a few years, long enough for us to plant a church and school of missions and leave it to the pastor while we moved to Africa. Our intention was to pass the ministry we were planting on to him. The jealousy came to a head while we were in Mozambique. It all started one day when our neighbors in Mexico contacted us saying that the pastor who owned the building had thrown all of our personal things out into the street. We also found out that he had approached our small team of 3 missionaries and church and tried to convince them that Olivia and I were not good leaders and they should follow him. When everyone told him no, that they were serving with us, he became furious. The missionaries went out of town for a weekend to visit family and when they returned to Reynosa, they were shocked to find their possessions had also been thrown out into the street. They called me asking what to do. We were heartbroken to hear this, I truly thought this man was my friend. For the first time in ministry, Olivia and I both felt the bitter sting of betrayal. It hurt us deeply. We sat in our room after receiving this call, shocked and unsure what to do. We began to honestly question whether we had made a mistake in going to Reynosa and whether we should even return, after all we had other options within Mexico and many other places. But as we prayed the Lord strongly reminded us that we needed to make the decision to obey Him regardless of whether anyone wanted us there or not. No man had called us, it was God who had brought us there. Then the Lord spoke a word to us that we were not expecting. He told us that we needed to commit to live in Mexico and specifically in Reynosa, until we died or until He moved us. It's one thing to commit for life to a place where you feel loved, accepted and successful, it is quite another to commit for life to serve in a place where you have been hurt, rejected and betrayed. We both wept, knowing how hard this would be but we were committed to the Lord to obey Him no matter the cost.

The apostle John had a vision of Jesus while he was in prison on the Isle of Patmos. By this point in his life, John had suffered greatly for his faith in Christ and was nearing the end of his life when Jesus gave him a final assignment to write down the revelation he received.

> Then I turned to see the voice that was speaking to me, and on turning I saw seven golden lampstands, and in the midst of the lampstands one like a son of man, clothed with a long robe and with a golden sash around his chest. The hairs of his head were white, like white wool, like snow. His eyes were like a flame of fire, his feet were like burnished bronze, refined in a furnace, and his voice was like the roar of many waters. In his right hand he held seven stars, from his mouth came a sharp two-edged sword, and his face was like the sun shining in full strength. When I saw him, I fell at his feet as though dead. But he laid his right hand on me, saying, "Fear not, I am the first and the last, and the living one. I died, and behold I am alive forevermore, and I have the keys of Death and Hades."
>
> Revelation 1:12-18

When we read this passage, it is easy to forget that John had been one of Jesus' closest earthly friends. He knew Jesus in the flesh as well as anyone ever had—he was there at the transfiguration, he was there at the crucifixion and he was there to see Jesus taken away to heaven. Yet even with all his personal experience as Jesus' friend, when he saw Jesus as the eternal king he was overcome and fell down before the Lord as a dead man. I have heard believers say that when they get to heaven they are going to ask Jesus specific questions... usually having to do with injustice or things they feel were unfair. In light of Scripture, these sorts of commentaries seem ridiculous. When we truly encounter the risen Jesus, the only thing we will be able to do is worship and obey Him!

After leaving Mozambique, we returned to Reynosa and tried to reconcile with the pastor. He refused, unless we worked under his direct control. We have never had a problem with biblical submission but knew that this man was not a healthy leader. We knew that it would never be possible to trust him and work together so we said goodbye. We spoke to our church leaders and offered for them to continue working with him, but no one was willing to. So we began to search for a place to move our church. We had been ministering in the garbage dump and decided to simply begin meeting for church there in the dump. During that time a friend of ours who is a local businessman in Reynosa met with us. He had heard what had happened and asked us what we needed. We told him how we were homeless and without money and needed a place to live. He took us to an apartment complex he owned and gave our missionary team 2 units to live in for free. We threw ourselves into ministry and began to expand our church planting efforts into more cities in Mexico.

Every week our church would go into the dump and have a service with the people who made a living picking things to sell from the mounds of trash. Many of them ended up there because of addictions and others had simply never known anything else. The needs of the people were tremendous but because we did not have much money, we did not know how we could help. One day the Lord told us to feed people in the dump. We did not know how since we did not have much money. He gave us a simple plan to buy what we would normally eat and plus a bit more and then divide our food and share it with the poor. We began with peanut butter sandwiches and bologna sandwiches. We watched week-by-week as God took our offering and multiplied it so that there was always enough food for both us and the people. A few months later, a man from the USA came to visit us and see our ministry in the dump. Afterwards he asked us if we wanted some beans. We thanked him and accepted his offer. A few days later I got a call asking where we could unload a semi-truck of beans and rice for our ministry. Since that time, we have distributed millions of meals and continue to help feed thousands of families in Mexico and other countries around the world.

Preaching at the Iris Global Bible School in Pemba, Mozambique.

With the help of our partners around the world, we have been able to help provide food to thousands of families in Mexico as well as other nations who were affected by violence, floods, earthquakes, and the pandemic.

Huge thanks to our partners, Rick Caywood Ministries, Ed Erwin, Power Ministries and Border Mission for helping us to feed thousands of families in Mexico.

Late nights unloading food supplies by hand!

Mobile feeding centers.

CHAPTER 12

THE BURNING ONES

The spiritual realm is more real than what we can see. Sometimes, however, God gives us a glimpse into what is occurring in this unseen realm. As I have walked with the Lord over the years, I have become keenly aware of the angelic activity occurring around me. In 2014, we hosted a medical team from our church in Brownwood, TX. We set up a clinic at a pastor friend's church in Reynosa. When we do free medical clinics, we have nurses process the people and find out what they need. Then while they wait to see the doctors, our ministry team shares the gospel with them and prays for them. We make it very clear that this has nothing to do with their medical treatment and that we would never want to manipulate them into accepting Jesus. In the early afternoon, a young mother brought a little boy into our clinic. She was covered in tattoos and had never come into an evangelical church before. Her son had a severe speech problem and had never learned to speak. He could make certain sounds but they were completely unintelligible. He was for all practical purposes mute. Our team began to pray for him and as they did the mother looked at her son with a panicked expression and audibly gasped for air. She took several steps back and fell into a chair screaming and sobbing. Meanwhile the little boy began to speak Spanish words clearly and communicate with the people around him. The mother embraced her son sobbing. After she regained her composure, she began to share with our team what had just happened. As the team had been praying for her son, she had seen a large angel walk into the room through the wall. The angel walked up to her son and touched his lips, and the moment he touched his lips was when the boy began to speak. The boy continued talking and improving his speech over the next few hours. During that time, the woman and her son gave their hearts to Jesus.

> Above him were seraphim, each with six wings: With two wings they covered their faces, with two they covered their feet, and with two they were flying. And they were calling to one another: "Holy, holy, holy is the LORD Almighty; the whole earth is full of his glory."
>
> Isaiah 6:2-3, NIV

When Isaiah encountered the Lord, he saw also burning angelic beings he referred to as *seraphim*. The word seraphim is a unique Hebrew word used to describe these otherworldly, heavenly beings from Isaiah's vision. This word is derived from the word *seraph* which means "burning or fiery"; so the word seraphim means "burning ones." This word is only used like this in Isaiah 6. I cannot imagine the struggle that Isaiah faced trying to express what he was seeing in his vision in human language. As he looked upon these burning creatures, he probably struggled immensely to describe what he saw. He hears these fiery heavenly beings crying out and worshipping the Lord on the throne. Their mighty, holy worship literally shook everything that Isaiah could see. As they worshipped the Lord, they cried out "Holy, holy, holy is the LORD Almighty; the whole earth is full of his glory." Isaiah is careful to explain the position that these powerful burning beings took before the presence of the Lord: with two wings they covered their faces, with two they covered their feet, and with two they were flying.

I believe that the reason the seraphim covered their face was so that the young prophet would not be distracted by their own beauty. The seraphim demonstrated beautiful humility in the presence of the Lord. One thing I have learned is that the closer you grow to Jesus the more you begin the disappear into His glory. As John the Baptist said when he saw Jesus, "I must decrease and he must increase." One excellent test to know whether you are Christ-focused or self-focused will occur when the Lord tells you to do something that people in your life may dislike. The fear of man stops many Christians from burning with the fire of the Holy Spirit because they are scared of what others may think if they step out in faith.

In our early days in Mexico, my wife and I were invited to minister in the southern part of the country. We spent several weeks ministering in many different types of churches. We saw God do many miracles. We did not speak Spanish yet, so the church invited an interpreter. As I met with the interpreter before the service it became obvious that we did not have the same beliefs regarding the gifts of the Holy Spirit. He was on staff at a conservative church that did not teach about the gifts or allow these things to happen in their fellowship meetings. I was very nervous; I did not want to offend this man and for a moment I considered changing my style of ministry and message for the night. Immediately, I heard the Holy Spirit command me not to hold back but to be myself and allow Him to flow through me. I repented for even considering bowing to the fear of man and prepared myself for the service. That night after the worship I was invited up to preach, and as I often do, I knelt down and invited the congregation to join me in worship. I began to sing in tongues and the Holy Spirit began to crash in. My wife later told me that my poor interpreter looked incredibly nervous to be associated with this crazy preacher. As we worshiped, the Lord began to give me words of knowledge about things He wanted to heal that night. The Holy Spirit showed me that there was someone there with a spirit of depression that had considered suicide and that God wanted to set that person free. A lady walked up to the front with tears streaming down her face. My interpreter, my wife, and I came up to her and began to minister to her. I asked her if she needed to forgive anyone. She pointed to my interpreter. I looked at him slightly confused and saw tears streaming down his face. This was his wife. She began to confess that she was in the process of filing for divorce and was planning to submit the papers the next morning. They wept and embraced each other as we cast out the demons of suicide and depression that she had struggled with for many years. That night the Lord taught me a lesson, to never hold back even a little bit but to allow Him to move in every situation. True humility actually makes us bolder than we could ever imagine because it is motivated by pleasing God rather than pleasing man. It also protects us from the pitfall of pride. The seraphim covered their faces because they did not want to distract Isaiah from the one sitting on the throne.

The seraphim also covered their feet. In the culture of the Old Testament, and in the Middle East to this day, it is a horrible insult to show the bottom of your feet or shoes because the bottom of the feet represent uncleanness or impurity. The seraphim covered their feet in God's presence because they understood better than anyone the holiness of the one who sat on the throne. Oftentimes holiness is preached as a series of rules. Holiness is much more than religious restrictions.

The word for holiness in Hebrew is *qodesh* which means set apart or consecrated for a holy purpose. We were created to live holy lives but sin distorts and perverts what God intended to be set apart for Himself. If we want to know what holiness looks like then we need to look back to the original design of how God made us. Adam and Eve were not created to sin. They were created to be set apart and walk with God. Sin took away their purpose and robbed them of their true destiny. When Christ was born into this world, he walked in a human body just like you and I but without the defilement of sin. He was the very definition of holy. As new covenant believers we are made holy by our covenant, which has been made possible by the death and resurrection of Christ. It was His atonement on the cross that cleanses us from the stain of sin and sets us free to fulfill our original design to walk with God and worship Him. His blood will never lose its power to save and transform us!

Once a team from our ministry was doing an outreach in the red-light district in Reynosa. In many border towns there are specifically designated prostitution zones where many Americans come to party. As our team was prayer walking, we came across a young prostitute who saw us and began to cry. The client she had with her ran off as we approached. I walked up to her and in English began to prophesy, "Thus saith the Lord, I want my daughter back." Three times I repeated these words. I was feeling very foolish, after all why should I speak in such old religious sounding language and in English no less? As we prayed for her, she fell to the ground weeping. After she regained her composure, she began to tell us her story. She was an American who was a backslidden youth pastor from the United Pentecostal church. We were dumbfounded by this, and asked her why she was there. She wept and told us that she had fallen in sin and people at her church told her that since she had fallen away, she was going to hell. She thought to herself, if I am going to hell, I might as well make money doing it. And through a series of bad decisions had decided to become a prostitute and ended up in Mexico selling her body. We explained that the grace of God could redeem her from her sin and guilt and make her holy. We could see hope in her eyes for the first time as she heard the true gospel of grace. She left the brothel with us that day and allowed us to minister to her. No one can be saved by simply following external rules. We need an inner working of the Holy Spirit in order to be transformed. Man-made rules can change the exterior of a person but only the Holy Spirit can change a person's heart.

The seraphim carried themselves in a very distinct way in the presence of the King. They did not sit or stand; instead they flew. I believe this speaks to a great need each of us have to be ready in season and out of season to receive orders from our king. In the same way if we are to burn with His glory, we must also remain sensitive to the Holy Spirit's leading. This is the key for accessing the miraculous power of God in our daily lives. Even Jesus modeled this kind of dependence on the Father in His life and ministry.

> So Jesus said to them, 'Truly, truly, I say to you, the Son can do nothing of his own accord, but only what he sees the Father doing. For whatever the Father does, that the Son does likewise.'
>
> John 5:19

Jesus made it clear to His followers that even though He was the Son of God, He did nothing apart from His Father. This verse offers us a unique insight into the intimate interdependent relationship between each member of the Trinity. This enables us to read the gospels in a new way when we have the constant horizontal dialogue between Jesus and His Father in mind. It truly adds so much depth to Jesus' methods in which He chose to heal people. Jesus did not use the same exact model or prayers to heal the sick. Sometimes He would declare, sometimes He would touch them. One blind man He touched, the other He spit in his eyes, another He spit in the mud and put the mud in his eyes. The reason He never did things the same way twice was because He was being moved by the Holy Spirit.

The Lord illustrated this to me in a powerful way in 2012 when I was ministering at a crusade in Haiti. We had been invited to come to Haiti to do an evangelistic campaign and pastors conference in the northern city of Jacamel. Haiti is a very unstable country in the Caribbean with strong cultural undercurrents of witchcraft. For a week we did training for local pastors and leaders in the morning and evangelistic meetings in the local soccer fields in the evening. The first night we preached but not much happened. There were a few sick people healed and a few gave their lives to the Lord but not many in comparison to the number of people there were. The next morning at the pastors meeting I shared a word about repentance and holiness. We asked the pastors to close their eyes and raise their hands if they were currently committing adultery, stealing money, and/or practicing witchcraft in their churches. As we went down this list of sins, one by one almost half of the pastors in the room raised their hands. The Holy Spirit fell on the place and many pastors were openly weeping and repenting for their sins. That night at the campaign the anointing of God came strongly into the meeting. Five blind people were healed publicly in front of the crowd. As I was praying for one of the blind women, I heard the Lord speak to me:

"Spit in her eyes."

I was a bit taken aback and tried to ignore that voice. I laid hands on the woman's eyes and continued to pray, but still nothing happened.

Again, I heard the Lord say, "Spit in her eyes."

I was becoming more and more frustrated and angrily replied back to the Lord under my breath "No! I will not do that."

Again, I heard the Lord say this time louder and stronger than before, "Spit in her eyes!"

I finally obeyed, and spit into my hands and touched her eyes. Immediately, I took my hands off her eyes and saw as a big smile came across her face. She screamed, "Light! Light! I can see the light!" Her vision was completely restored in moments. I fell to my knees and repented of my attitude and stubborn pride.

There is not a formula for miracles or for our walk with God. The Holy Spirit is a person. He called us to walk in a relationship of obedience with Him. He is continually inviting us deeper to encounter Him and be moved and led by His Spirit.

God is calling us to burn for His glory but in order to sustain this fire we must commit to walk in a humility that will never try to rob Him of His glory. We must walk in holiness that comes from being covered by the blood of Jesus, and mobility that keeps us ready to follow the Holy Spirit's leading no matter what the cost.

Young boy who was healed of muteness and began to speak clearly.

Preaching the gospel in open air meetings in Haiti.

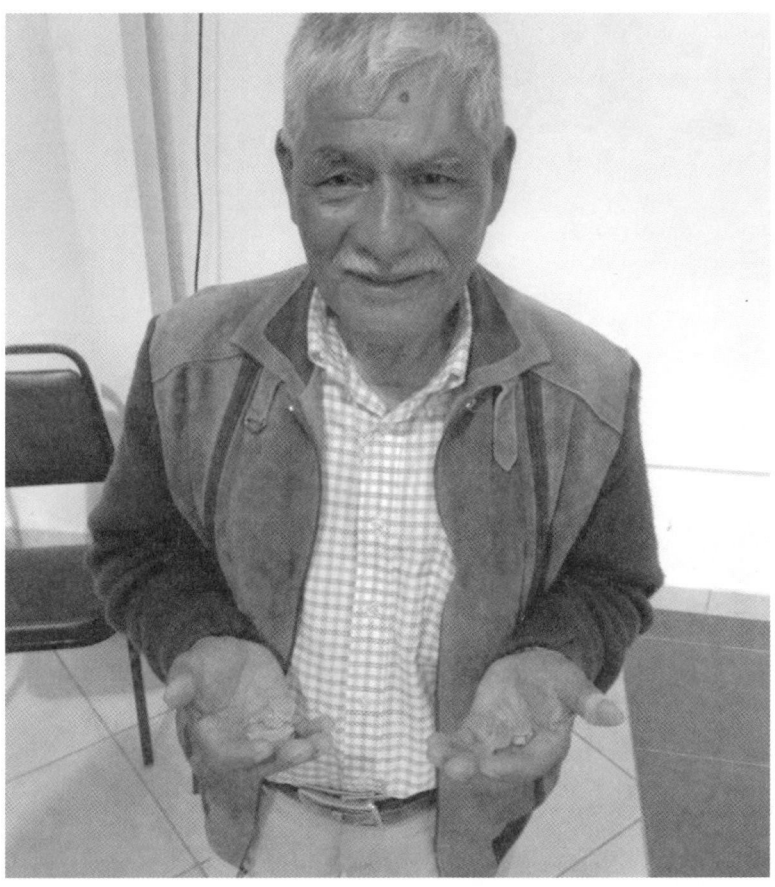

This man was healed of a severe hearing problem. After receiving prayer, he could hear perfectly without his hearing aids.

CHAPTER 13

A DEAD MAN

Moving to Mexico was a challenge for me, because my primary calling is to establish churches. In a nation like Mexico, however, there were already many churches. I felt out of place on the border and questioned God why he would send me here. Then as I got to know other churches, I began to understand that what I had experienced with the betrayal and subsequent lack of trust was a common theme in most churches in the region where I lived. Church splits were common as leaders with orphaned spirits fought for significance and control of resources. There was a lot of corruption, immorality and distrust among pastors. With this revelation ringing in my spirit, I began to pray with groups of pastors asking God to send revival to the church. During one of these prayer meetings, God spoke clearly to me and asked me a series of questions.

He said, "Are you ready for revival? If I send three thousand people to you tomorrow who desire to be saved and discipled are you ready to receive them? Do you know any church who is?"

These questions left me speechless as I sat in the room full of praying pastors. I began weeping, saying to the Lord that no, we are not ready for revival. I wept bitter tears as I realized that we were asking for something without truly believing we would receive it.

As I knelt there repenting, I heard the Lord say to me, "I desire to build a new wineskin to receive the new wine of my Spirit. This new wineskin will be missionaries, pastors, leaders and church members with healed hearts who can carry a move of My Spirit."

> At the sound of their voices the doorposts and thresholds shook and the temple was filled with smoke. "Woe to me!" I cried. "I am ruined! For I am a man of unclean lips, and I live among a people of unclean lips, and my eyes have seen the King, the LORD Almighty."
>
> Isaiah 6:4-5, NIV

Sometimes revival does not come as we expect it to. Around the world believers are praying for revival but oftentimes they do not have a Biblical understanding of what true revival implies. Before God can trust us with the full, raw power of His Spirit, He needs to shake us to our core. In Isaiah's heavenly encounter, the doorpost and thresholds shook. I can imagine that Isaiah was shaking as well! In the old days, when someone was searching for gold in a river they would scoop out sand, dirt and rocks from the river bank and then shake it in a pan. This process of "panning" allows the person searching to wash away the dirt so that the gold could be brought to the surface. In the same way, God's presence shakes us as believers so that whatever can be shaken, will be shaken away so that only that which is of Him remains. Oftentimes because we do not understand what true revival looks like we do not know how to prepare ourselves for a move of the Holy Spirit.

While we were in Mozambique, we had the opportunity to connect with a missionary named Dan Slade, the leader of the network of churches that had been birthed out of the Toronto revival (The Toronto Blessing). While we were speaking to him, he felt the Lord leading him to invite Olivia and I to come to their annual conference. They covered our flights and brought us to their church in Canada. The Toronto Blessing was a powerful revival in the 90s that started in a small church near the airport. The Holy Spirit began to be poured out in such powerful ways that people came from all around the world to encounter God in the church. They held nightly meetings for 10 years and during that time they estimate that somewhere around 5 million people came and were touched in these services. This revival was focused on the manifest power of the Holy Spirit, this electric atmosphere, combined with a strong revelation of the Father heart of God and inner healing that resulted in thousands of lives being transformed. Although they no longer have nightly meetings, the manifest presence of God is still incredibly strong in this church. When we arrived in Toronto, it became painfully obvious to me how badly I needed to receive healing of the heart. I was still struggling with unforgiveness because of hurts I had experienced. I would often joke that I loved people but did not trust anyone. As I laid down on the floor during worship in the beautiful Toronto church, I felt the Lord bringing to my memory every person who I needed to forgive. Much of the inner healing the happens in revival occurs during times of deep worship. During this conference, we encountered precious spiritual mothers and fathers who gathered around us and prayed for us. We both spent many hours where we could not get off the floor. People often ask me, "Why do people fall down under the power of God?" I think the answer is twofold. One, because it is a tangible physical reaction to encountering the Almighty. Two, because most of us are so busy running around that God needs to put us on the ground to deal with the issues of our heart.

In my experience, inner healing is not always a one-time experience. Sometimes unexplained physical sickness is the result of a deeper problem of the heart. Once while ministering in a small village near Piedras Negras, Mexico, an elderly woman walked slowly and painfully into the church. Our team was there doing an outreach. As we were getting started, I saw her limp up to the front pew slowly, supported only by her cane. At the end of the service we called for people to come and receive prayer for healing. She came and sat down on the front row. We gathered around her and began to pray. She had suffered a stroke which had paralyzed her body on one side and left one hand curled up, permanently cradled against her chest. Despite our fervent prayers nothing seemed to be happening. Suddenly the Lord spoke to me and said, "Ask her if she has anyone she needs to forgive." I knelt down and asked her the question. She began to weep and talk about how she needed to forgive her daughter. We asked her where her daughter was and she pointed to a woman in the back. We invited the woman to the front and the mother asked forgiveness from her daughter. She began to weep and asked her mother for forgiveness in return. As they wept and embraced each other her hand with contorted and frozen fingers suddenly began to move. She was healed that night as she chose to forgive. She walked out carrying her cane!

God often deals with our issues in layers. Difficult situations such as betrayal can cause new wounds. But once you have encountered the Healer it becomes increasingly easier for you to trust Him and run back to Him for healing as new situations arise. When Isaiah encountered God, he cried out and said, "I am ruined." Some translations say, "I am a dead man!" I believe this is probably the most accurate description of what happened to Isaiah that day. In the presence of God, Isaiah became acutely aware of his own problems and the depth of his need for God. For Isaiah, the problem he became aware of was that his lips were unclean. Perhaps Isaiah was prone to cussing fits, or maybe his words were sarcastic, bitter, or angry. Regardless of the specifics, this problem came boiling up to the surface when Isaiah encountered God. Inner healing is a natural outcome of encountering a Holy God!

Once while my wife and I were ministering at a church in Quintana Roo, Mexico, a woman came into the meeting who was very skeptical of my ministry. She was the sister of one of the pastors in the church. She was a member of a very conservative church that did not believe in the modern moving of the Holy Spirit. She needed a healing in her body, so after a significant amount of convincing from her sister she agreed to attend the meeting. She told her sister however, that if I pushed her down when I prayed for her, she would leave and never come back to a charismatic church again. Her sister did not tell me this, nor introduce me to her until after the service. That night during the service, I called up people who needed healing in their body. She came to the front and joined the line of people. As she closed her eyes in prayer, she felt a large hand grab her forehead and shove her down to the ground. No one caught her and she hit the concrete floor hard. She opened her eyes, furious at me for pushing her down, but then realized that I was on the opposite side of the room praying for other people. No one had caught her because no one had physically prayed for her. She tried to get up, but was unable to. In that moment she realized that this was God putting her down on the floor. While she laid there, God Himself ministered to her and broke down all of her resistance to the Holy Spirit and healed her. That woman was baptized in the Holy Spirit and left the church completely different than when she arrived.

> Now when it was evening, the disciples came to him and said, "This is a desolate place, and the day is now over; send the crowds away to go into the villages and buy food for themselves." But Jesus said, "They need not go away; you give them something to eat." They said to him, "We have only five loaves here and two fish." And he said, "Bring them here to me." Then he ordered the crowds to sit down on the grass, and taking the five loaves and the two fish, he looked up to heaven and said a blessing. Then he broke the loaves and gave them to the disciples, and the disciples gave them to the crowds.
>
> Matthew 14:15-19

When Jesus saw the hunger of the crowd, He asked the disciples what they had. God is not interested in what we do not have, but in what we do have. Many times, when God calls us to do something we have a lot of excuses about why we cannot do what He said to do because we don't have money, knowledge, experience, training etc.,— you can fill in the blank. Jesus wants to multiply our lives so that we will be fruitful for Him. The disciples gave Jesus the loaves and fish, he took them in His hands, gave thanks for them and broke the loaves. Thankfulness to God brings supernatural multiplication to our lives. In our ministry we have seen God bring about supernatural multiplication of our resources to further the Kingdom. In Juarez, during the height of the drug wars our team was invited to come and share in the community centers throughout the city. These community centers are a government program that provide services to the community. The desire of the government officials who invited us was that we could minister to at-risk youth with the hope that they would not grow up to join the gangs that plagued the city. We agreed on the condition that we could fully preach the gospel and not just give talks about moral values. The administration reluctantly agreed on the condition that we also give school supplies to the children. They told us to expect approximately 1,000 children. When our team arrived in Juarez, we purchased enough school supplies to make 1,700 bags. The next day, however, we found out that the opportunity had expanded to over 20 community centers and thousands of children. We had no idea what to do, we did not have money for more supplies. We prayed over the bags and gave thanks to God for the opportunity. The first two days we thought we had given out all of the bags but when we returned to the ministry base, we found that there were more. Every day we thought we had given out everything only to discover that the bags were multiplying as fast as we could give them out. We kept track of how many bags were given out at each distribution and were amazed to find that although we had only brought 1,700 bags, we had given out well over 4,000 and still had bags left over! During that time many children and parents gave their lives to Jesus along with many of the staff.

Jesus also took the loaves and fish and broke them. In my opinion, being broken by the Lord is a prerequisite for supernatural multiplication. The breaking of the Lord is different than the breaking of the world. The world breaks and destroys lives whereas Jesus takes us like soft clay in His hands and applies His pressure to break us free from our current form and remake us according to His will and image. Without His breaking, we cannot experience His healing.

I do not believe that this breaking means that God sends sickness or disease upon us to teach us a lesson. I believe that the true breaking we need is a breaking and remaking in His glorious presence. The breaking results in our healing, and the healing then allows us to be used by God to multiply that which we have received in the lives of others.

Much of the church is stuck because they have not allowed Jesus to heal their wounds. The Bible says that every creature should multiply after its own kind. This means that you multiply what you are, not just what you know. God desires to use us but He wants to first heal us and deliver us so that he can multiply our healing instead of multiplying our dysfunction. This is the wineskin that the Father is looking for to host a move of His Holy Spirit around the world.

What area in your life is holding you back from answering His call? For Isaiah, it was his tongue. The first step is to be honest with the Lord and allow Him to bring the healing we need.

Crying out for more!

Our team ministering to kids in open air children's campaigns.

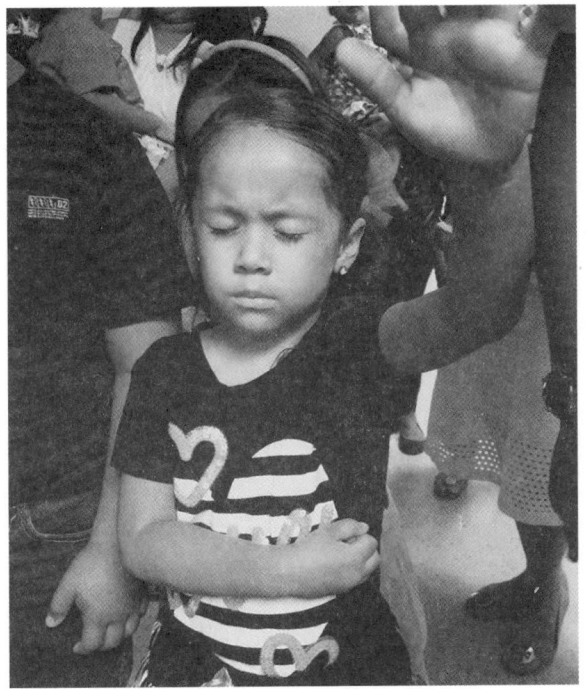

The true heart of worship!

CHAPTER 14

THE FIRE OF TESTING

After leaving Toronto, Olivia and I were invited to a conference for the International School of Ministry in California. We arrived excited to be a part of this incredible event with leaders from around the world. On the first night however, I began to feel sick and got a sharp pain in my side. I continued to pray until the pain became unbearable. I have felt very close to death multiple times in my life, but this time I truly felt as though I was walking through the valley of the shadow. My wife took me to the hospital where the doctors confirmed that I had acute appendicitis. We did not have insurance and I knew the cost of medical treatment in the USA. I begged the doctors to let me leave and go back to Mexico so we could afford the treatment but because my appendix was about to rupture, they refused. They rushed me in for an emergency surgery. As I was being prepped for surgery, I was preaching to everyone around me; after all if these were going to be my final moments, I wanted to be found faithful. I spent time praying for the nurses and doctors and sharing the gospel with them.

> Then one of the seraphim flew to me, having in his hand a burning coal that he had taken with tongs from the altar. And he touched my mouth and said: "Behold, this has touched your lips; your guilt is taken away, and your sin atoned for."
>
> Isaiah 6:6-7

Oftentimes when we powerfully encounter the Lord, the enemy comes against us to test our resolve and commitment to serve the Lord. I am a firm believer in the goodness of God. He is so good that He is utterly incapable of evil. Our enemy the devil on the other hand, is completely incapable of true love or goodness. He constantly seeks opportunity to destroy the people of God. He has no power to remove us from God's will. His power is limited and his days are numbered. His only chance for success is to convince us to voluntarily remove ourselves from God's will and plan for our lives.

As I laid on the bed awaiting surgery, I could hear the lying whispers of the enemy.

"You are a failure, just give up and die. What kind of God do you serve who heals the multitudes but refuses to heal you?" I was in such pain, all I could do was worship and pray in tongues.

I came out of the surgery and began the recovery process. After two weeks, the doctors cleared me to travel. However, we still had the problem about how we would pay for this surgery. The hospital bill totaled out to $32,000. The surgeon who I had ministered to in the prep room had been so touched that he decided to do his portion of the surgery for free. The anesthesiologist who I had also ministered to cut his bill in half. This still left us with a huge bill from the hospital itself. We had no idea what to do and thought that perhaps we would have to leave Mexico to find work and pay off our debt.

There are moments in our lives when our faith is strong and the path ahead seems clear. Then there are other moments when there simply seems to be no good way forward, and we feel like complete failures. This was the condition where I felt myself at during this time. I would try to remind myself of the words I had received from the Lord and the powerful things He had done and spoken, but I could not shake the thought that I had nothing to show for my first year in Mexico. After I was cleared to fly, I returned to my family farm in Waxahachie, Texas to recover. I had never felt so tired and discouraged in my life. I tried my best to put on a good face as my dad and I discussed normal small-town things such as ranching, cattle and the last time it rained. It was a refreshing break from the chaos that had been the past year of my life. I was afraid to share about how hard things had been for Olivia and I. After all, every son who leaves home wants his father to see that he is a "success." I knew my father loved me unconditionally but deep inside I feared that he would come to see me as a failure. So there I sat, thousands of dollars in debt, with little consistent support. I had stepped out in faith and moved to Mexico, and there I was almost a year later with very little to show for my effort. I could not concentrate on what my father was saying, all I could hear was a nagging voice of the devil bombarding my thoughts:

"You are a failure. You will always be a failure. You just need to quit."

It was a demonic thought; I had heard it many times before, but there in my childhood home it seemed louder than ever. As I sat there under this intense onslaught of discouraging thoughts, I reached my breaking point. I suddenly couldn't take it any longer and began to weep. My dad is not a very emotional man, he is typically very quiet. He has never served in ministry although he loves the Lord with a deep and humble faith that has always inspired me. As hot tears ran down my face, I tried to hide the fact that I was crying—this was not manly behavior after all. As I hid my face in my hands I heard my father jump out of his chair and run toward me, clearing the short space between our chairs in a few seconds. He reached down and wrapped his arms around me. I could hear his voice quivering with emotion as he said, "Son, I don't understand what you do or what you are going through now, but you are my son and I love you and I am so proud of you." He then began to pray for me asking God to comfort and help me. As he prayed, I suddenly heard the voice of the Lord saying, "My son, you are not a failure. What you feel now is but a fraction of the love I have for you."

For knowledge to become revelation it must make the journey from the head to the heart. I knew that God was a good Father who loved me, but deep inside I felt that any weakness on my part constituted failure that displeased Him. But as my father embraced me, I could feel the arms of the heavenly Father strengthening me and giving me courage not to quit the race.

On that day, God showed me what the love of the Father truly looks like through my dad. Sometimes we need more than anything else in our lives to experience the hug of our heavenly Father. In the Bible, the difference between the prodigal son and the older brother was the attitude in which they approached the father. The younger brother knew he had messed up and deserved nothing. He gratefully received his father's embrace and was healed and restored.

The older brother, however, resisted his father's embrace because of his own self-righteousness. He was so bound up in a works mentality and self-reliance that he could not admit to himself or his father that he also had a problem. This bottled-up frustration boiled over in anger at his father's grace towards his brother. The love of our heavenly Father is unconditional; it restores us and lifts us up. A few days later as my wife and I made plans to return to Mexico, we got a call from the hospital billing department. They said that they had reviewed our case and that my bill had now been covered in full by a donor foundation.

Jesus never promised that we would have it easy when we followed Him. In fact, He promised that,

> "...in this world you will have trouble. But take heart! For I have overcome the world."
>
> John 16:33, NIV

This phrase "take heart" means to have courageous hope in Christ and believe by faith in what Jesus has already done as we wait for the victory of Jesus to be manifested and change the reality of our circumstances. Faith is hope that has been tested and refined in the fire of adversity. It is much more than simply good thoughts or feelings.

> Now faith is the substance of things hoped for the evidence of things not seen.
>
> Hebrews 11:1, NKJV

The fire takes our knowledge of God's Word and promises and test that hope to see if we truly believe what we say we believe. This process converts our knowledge into revelation as our faith in God becomes something tested and proven that enables us to withstand future storms as we look back to the faithfulness of God in our past.

CHAPTER 15

THE HEARTBEAT OF THE LORD

We returned to Mexico and continued to see God's power poured out in amazing ways. We began to plant churches and serve the poor. Olivia and I knew that in order for us to help prepare the church in Mexico for a new wave of His Spirit, we needed more training in inner healing. We returned again to Catch The Fire Church in Toronto the following year and during worship I was taken by the Lord into an open vision that would forever change my life and ministry. In this vision, I saw myself standing in a wheat field with a beautiful bountiful harvest in every direction as far as the eye could see. I was standing with an old-fashioned sickle in the middle of the wheat working as hard as I could but with very little success. I threw the sickle down and fell to the ground weeping, saying, "It's too much! It's too much!" Suddenly I was in the vision, not just seeing it as an observer but actually living it as though I was there. I saw heaven open and a ball of fire fall from heaven and hit me in the chest. I was completely engulfed in this fire. Out of the fire the Lord spoke to me and asked me a question: "Do you want to build your ministry, or do you want to give birth to a movement?" I realized in that moment that my ministry was everything I had been able to do up until that point, but he was asking me if I was willing to be part of something new. "Yes! I screamed! Whatever it takes!" As those words left my lips, I saw giant combine tractors falling out of heaven and landing in different parts of the field, first dozens of tractors then hundreds and eventually thousands. They began to work together and bring in the harvest at an incredible rate. The Lord then said to me, "Dedicate yourself to prayer and fasting and stay in My fire."

> Then I heard the voice of the Lord saying, "Whom shall I send? And who will go for us?" And I said, "Here am I. Send me!."
>
> Isaiah 6:8, NIV

In Isaiah's vision he had seen and heard incredible things: angels, glory, even the Lord Himself sitting on a throne. But it wasn't until he was touched by the fire in the vision, that he actually began to hear the quiet voice of God. Oftentimes we are waiting for a booming voice to inform us of God's will, while God is steadily inviting us to come close and hear his heartbeat.

The prophet Elijah also encountered the quiet voice of the Lord during a time of great discouragement in his life.

> And he said, "Go out and stand on the mount before the Lord." And behold, the Lord passed by, and a great and strong wind tore the mountains and broke in pieces the rocks before the Lord, but the Lord was not in the wind. And after the wind an earthquake, but the Lord was not in the earthquake. And after the earthquake a fire, but the Lord was not in the fire. And after the fire the sound of a low whisper. And when Elijah heard it, he wrapped his face in his cloak and went out and stood at the entrance of the cave. And behold, there came a voice to him and said, "What are you doing here, Elijah?."
>
> I Kings 19:11-13

We tend to judge our spiritual experience by how sensational the experience was. As I have had the privilege of traveling and speaking in revival meetings around the world, I have met people who tend to jump from conference to conference looking for spiritual experiences. I treasure each and every way that God chooses to touch me. I love the manifestations of His Spirit, the fire, and the shaking that comes when His manifest glory enters the room. However, as I have walked with Him over the years, I have come to see that the purpose of these manifestations is simply to get our attention so that we can hear His still small voice. I believe what happened in Isaiah's vision was that after being touched by the fire his ears were opened to hear a conversation between the Father, Son and Holy Spirit asking the question, "Whom shall I send? And who will go for us?" Overhearing this call provided unique insight for Isaiah into the heart's desire of the Lord regarding the people of Israel who were spiritually blind and deaf, much like Isaiah had been before he was touched by the fire.

We live in a world of people who are deaf to hearing God and need the power of the Holy Spirit to open their ears to hear of His love. Once while ministering in a remote village in South Sudan near the Congo border, the Lord illustrated this point to me through a powerful miracle. I went with a team of local pastors from the Bible college to minister to people in the market. We gathered a little crowd in the market of mostly drunk men and began to preach to them. We asked if anyone wanted to surrender their lives to Jesus and no one responded. I then asked if anyone needed healing. One man replied yes, that he had suffered from malaria and his body was aching badly. We laid hands on him and prayed. We watched his face fill with surprise as the pain and fever left his body. But still he was afraid to make a commitment to Christ in front of his drinking buddies. A very old man came up at that moment and asked us for prayer. He had suffered from a sharp pain in his chest for almost a year. We laid hands on him and began to pray. The pain left him almost immediately. He thanked us and asked us to please go and pray for the old blind woman in the village who had been sick for many years. We promised we would, and some of the locals agreed to show us the way to her house. We arrived at her house and found that she had likely suffered from a stroke or embolism during the war which had caused her to lose part of her brain function. She was blind, deaf, and had not been able to speak clearly for years. She could only lay on her little woven grass bed, unable to care for herself. It was an incredibly sad sight to see. The Bible school students tried to lead her to Christ but realized quickly that she could not hear or understand them. One then said, lets pray for God to comfort her and her family. "No," I replied, "We need to pray for God to heal her." Even I was a bit shocked by the forcefulness and confidence of the words that came out of my mouth. The local believers stepped out of the way and watched as I began to pray for healing. As I laid hands on her and began to pray, she began to speak. First softly, then with more strength. In the Kakwa language she said that something had popped in her head.

The local believers came close and began to pray for her with me as well. We asked her to sit up, she replied that she could not. Her muscles had become too weak and atrophied. We helped her sit up anyway. We continued to pray for her, as I prayed for her legs, I felt her leg muscles growing stronger. We asked her to stand, she replied that she could not. We helped her up anyway. She stood shakily to her feet with several of us holding her up. We asked if she could walk. She said yes. Leaning on our arms, she began to take a few steps, at first weakly then with more and more strength. It was at that moment that I realized that she was blind. I asked her to pray for her eyes. I laid hands on her eyes and prayed and God opened her eyes! She looked at me and exclaimed in Arabic, "You are a white man!" After a few minutes she let go of the hands of the ones who had been supporting her and stepped out into the sunshine for the first time in many years! We then began to explain the gospel of Jesus to her stunned family. The entire family gave their lives to the Lord. That night at the church an uproar broke out as the same drunks from the market came to give their lives to Jesus because of the miracle God had done.

Many people think that finding the will of God for their lives is illusive or mysterious. The reality however, is that it is not complicated to know His will if you are willing to spend the time it takes to get to know His heart. The apostle John wrote differently than any of the other gospel writers. Theologians place the gospels of Matthew, Mark and Luke in a category of synoptic gospels, meaning they summarize neatly with much overlap the life and ministry of Jesus. The gospel of John is completely in a category of its own. Although it clearly tells the same story and does not contradict the other gospels, its overall tone differs greatly and reveals another aspect of the nature of Christ, not just a Savior for the Jews but as the Savior for all mankind.

I personally believe that the reason John's gospel differs from the others is because of the close personal relationship that John had with Jesus. John often referred to himself as the disciple whom Jesus loved and was in the inner circle of Jesus' friends. Their closeness was like that of a father and his child. At the Last Supper, John leaned back against Jesus' chest to ask Him who would betray Him, and at that moment Jesus revealed who it would be (John 13). Symbolically and literally, John had heard the heart of Jesus, while the others wrote the first three gospels as the Spirit inspired them from what they had seen Jesus do. John's gospel is unique because he wrote it as a love message to the world written from the perspective of one who had heard the heart of God. The first three gospels reveal the nature of Christ as Messiah, Savior and Redeemer. The book of John reveals the loving heart of Jesus to a world dying in sin.

In much the same way, I believe Isaiah's call was not simply an order issued from the voice of God, but an invitation directly from the heart of God. God is not looking for more servants to do His bidding. He is looking for those who truly love Him to come close and hear His heart for the lost and broken. Like Elijah, John, and Isaiah, God is inviting people to step so close to Him that we can hear His quiet voice and know the desires of His heart. Once we know what He wants for our lives, it becomes easier than ever to say, like Isaiah, "Here I am Lord, send me!"

Many believers make the error of trying to manipulate God into blessing their plans. This is a grave mistake because God's plans are always better than ours. The true way to find fulfillment in your calling is to get so close to Jesus that you hear what He desires to do then volunteer to be part of it.

People often ask, "What is revival?" There are lots of books written by men and women much wiser than me on the subject. My simple definition is this, revival is a sovereign move of the Holy Spirit that turns the hearts of the people toward the Father. The Holy Spirit comes to people who are hungry and positioned to receive Him in this way. His manifest presence leads to repentance, supernatural joy, healing and supernatural growth, both in numbers and individual maturity. The end result of this revival should then be waves of people being sent out carrying the message that was birthed from the heart of the Father. Revival rapidly accelerates the growth of new believers.

Once Olivia and I were ministering in the West African nation of Sierra Leone. While going door-to-door in the slum in the capital, Free Town, we came across a group of three men drinking and smoking. They invited me into their yard and asked what we were doing in their neighborhood. I began to share the gospel with them. They were touched by the message of Christ. They agreed that they wanted to follow Jesus. I led them in a prayer, and just as we finished a blind man came walking up. He had heard me speaking English and knew I must be a foreigner and thought he could get some money. I asked if I could pray for him, he replied yes. I then turned to the new converts who were now just a few minutes old in the faith and explained to them that Jesus did many miracles. And that he would send His Spirit to rest upon us to do the same miracles he did. They put down their beer bottles and laid hands on the man. We then asked the man, who had been completely blind for many years, if he could see. He had a shocked look on his face saying he could now see light. We prayed again for the man. He opened his eyes, this time he could see shapes but everything was blurry. We prayed again, this time he could see perfectly. The men were amazed, the formerly blind man also gave his life to the Lord. God is looking to shift our paradigm of what normal Christianity looks like. God chose to partner with these new believers for His Spirit to flow through them to heal a blind man. The gospel was illustrated beautifully to these men in a few minutes!

When I had this vision of the harvest, I felt that I was stepping into something that was beyond my abilities. I never imagined that I would be leading a movement of churches and birthing a missionary organization. We did not have a name for our ministry, but after this vision in Toronto, I knew that God was about to do something new and that we needed to prepare ourselves for supernatural growth. For that reason, I knew that we needed a name. We had used a couple of different names for churches we had planted, but none of them felt right in this new season. I prayed and asked the Lord to show us what to name this new thing that He was birthing. Yet despite weeks of prayer and brainstorming sessions, we could not find anything that seemed right. During this time, our small team continued to make the rounds to the different cities in Mexico where we worked training church leaders and laying the ground work for church planting. One day while visiting Laredo, the Lord woke me up in the middle of the night. I heard His voice clearly call out of the darkness, "Look up the word for 'called' in the Greek." I got out of bed and googled the word for "called" in Biblical Greek. It was the word *kaleo*. As soon as I saw this word, I felt excitement in my Spirit as I heard the Holy Spirit say, this is what I am calling you.

After that vision we began to experience exponential growth. Within just a few months of returning to Mexico our little team grew from a handful of missionaries in Reynosa to rapidly growing team of missionaries and church planters throughout Mexico, Texas, and Africa. People began to come from different nations to serve as missionaries in Mexico. Miracles began to break out like I had never seen before.

Once while our team was doing an open-air meeting in a fishing village in Mexico called Playa Bagdad, a woman came to the front for us to pray for her. She had a tumor protruding from her stomach the size of a softball. As we laid hands on her the power of God touched her and she suddenly fell backwards. The man who was catching her was part of the visiting team from Texas. He had not told any of us but many years ago he had injured his hand in an accident with a power saw. He had suffered nerve damage and could not move two of his fingers anymore. As he caught the women and lowered her to the ground, he felt fire go into his damaged hand. He realized that he had feeling again in his fingers and could move them again. As the woman laid on the ground, several women from our team gathered around her to pray. One of the women, a nurse named Hannah from Texas, had her hand on the tumor and suddenly felt the tumor disappear out from under her hand. She was surprised and began to feel around for the tumor but could not find it. It had completely disappeared. As a result of this miracle, we planted a new church in this village.

In one of our conferences a pastor named Juan Carlos attended with his family. He and his wife Veronica had two teenagers named Jair and Anita that came with their parents. The whole family was very touched by the Lord and Anita and Jair spent several hours on the floor on the first day under the power of the Holy Spirit. The next day, I saw them translating for the team who was visiting from the USA who spoke only English. I was surprised because I did not think that Jair or Anita could speak English. Later that day I approached them and asked them where they learned English, they replied that the day before they could only speak a few words of English that they had learned in school. But after being touched by the Lord, they got up off the floor and could understand everything the Americans were saying. After receiving this supernatural download of the English language, they could even translate. They can still speak and translate English to this very day.

This kind of supernatural move of the Holy Spirit also attracts the attention of people operating under demonic influence who come with the intention of disrupting and stopping the preaching of the gospel. Once while our team was ministering at an outdoor meeting in Reynosa, a man approached the platform. He looked normal but as he walked to the front, he seemed to hit an invisible wall and fell to his knees screaming. The team began to pray for him and cast demons out of him. After he had been set free, he just laid down, seemingly in shock at what had just happened. Shortly after, another man in the crowd fell down and began to scream. The ministry team began to pray for him and cast demons out of him as well. After the meeting the two men confessed that they were both witches and had come to the meeting to cast spells and disrupt the meeting. In worship, they both encountered the power of God and were powerfully set free and gave their lives to Jesus.

In 2018, we had the opportunity to host John Arnott, the pastor of the church that received the revival in Toronto, here in Reynosa, Mexico. During the service, a young woman approached the stage wanting to give a testimony. We asked her what happened. She replied that she had been healed of cancer. Sometimes people like to give a testimony "by faith" with the hope that what they are testifying about will come to pass. I understand the heart behind this; however, we have learned to be cautious to screen the people who give testimonies to make sure that there has been a verifiable change in their condition. We often send people back to their doctors to check that something has changed. We asked her how she knew she had been healed and she pointed to a wheelchair with a woman standing behind it sobbing and said, "That is my wheelchair, my mother pushed me into this meeting because I could not stand up." She went on to testify that she had a very aggressive form of ovarian cancer that had metastasized throughout her abdomen, leaving her in constant pain. The doctors did not give her any hope but as she sat there in the service, she felt fire come into her body suddenly and felt as though something pushed her forcefully out of her wheelchair onto her feet. She was shocked as she looked around her to find that no one had touched her. As she stood up, she knew that she had been supernaturally healed because all of the pain had left her body. She felt her abdomen where the tumors had been just shortly before and could not find them.

As signs of revival began to explode around us, we stood in awe of the scale of the miracles we were seeing. My wife and I could not believe the supernatural growth. In 2018, we started our first school of missions in Reynosa for training missionaries. And later that same year, we started a church planting school to train new pastors who felt called to plant churches. We began to see people coming from around the world to be trained and sent out. As of 2021, we have seen hundreds of people from more than 30 different nations come not only to serve but also to encounter God here at our base in Reynosa. Many have been sent out to plant Kaleo churches in other nations around the world.

This woman was healed of a large tumor in her stomach, in Playa Bagdad, Mexico.

A few months after the woman was healed of the tumor in Playa Bagdad, another woman came to one of our meetings with a tumor in the same spot. We had the woman who had been healed pray for her and the younger woman's tumor instantly disappeared!

Revival meetings in the mountains of southern Mexico!

Fire night meetings in Reynosa, Mexico with John Arnott.

Revival meetings in Jojutla, Mexico with Heidi Baker.

In these revival meetings, the glory would fall and people would continue to worship through the night sometimes even camping out in the open fields.

Altar call for youth to give their lives to Christ.

Our first gathering of Kaleo missionaries in 2016, seeking the Lord's face together.

Kaleo Family Gathering 2019.

Kaleo Family Gathering 2020.

CHAPTER 16

SEEING AND PERCEIVING

In the year 2020, the world was struck with a horrible pandemic that took the lives of many people. The year began with much promise, many people prophesied about 2020 being a year of vision and revival. At the beginning of the year, I felt from the Lord that we would experience a new wave of His Spirit and that God would open our eyes to see with greater clarity. I thought I had an idea of what that might look like, only to discover later that I had no idea what all that word would entail in the days ahead. When news reached us of the pandemic, we were faced with the decision of what to do. I saw many pastor friends responding in opposite extremes, some with fear who shut down their churches without even being asked to, while others claimed with hubris that this was a fake pandemic. At that time we had our school of missions up and running with students from throughout Mexico and multiple other countries here at our base in

Reynosa. Many of our students were receiving calls and emails from their families saying they needed to return home. The USA announced during that time that the border between America and Mexico would be closing and that any Americans in Mexico needed to return to the USA or risk not being able to return for an indefinite amount of time. Our team was divided as to what our response should be. I felt the weight of these decisions looming heavily on my mind. I could see absolutely no perfect answer on what to do. In moments like this in my life I have learned the importance of developing a lifestyle of prayer and fasting. Fasting helps us to focus in on Jesus and allows Him to speak to us and give us direction and clarity for decisions we need to make. So, our team decided to fast for 8 days and seek the Lord's guidance and strategy for what to do. Sometimes the hardest thing about the walk of faith is to learn to look beyond the circumstances of our daily lives and see what Jesus is truly doing. We wanted to press in and truly hear what His will for us was and how to be victorious.

During this time of fasting, a man who has been a spiritual father to me for many years named Kelly Crenshaw called me and gave me a word from the Lord. He told us that God was about to give us a once in a lifetime opportunity in the middle of this pandemic and that we could not afford to miss what God would do in this time. This word was the answer I had been waiting for and seemed to shake away the confusion and fear that had bombarded my mind and made me feel paralyzed. The Lord downloaded a strategy to our team on how to grow during this time and be a conduit of blessing to the people around us who did not know where their next meal would come from. During the time of pandemic, an evil spirit of fear operated freely in the earth. People who I had always known to be people of faith, suddenly began to speak as though they had none. Others tried through brash talk to convince themselves and others that they were not afraid. The spirit of fear truly blinds us to the reality of heaven and convinces us to make decisions that are the opposite of faith. These decisions rooted in fear can even seem virtuous in the moment but can lead us down a very dark path. The key for victory during times of crisis in our lives is to press into the presence of Jesus and ask Him for spiritual vision and direction. This gives us the ability to walk resolutely with humble confidence because we know the one who is leading us.

> He said, "Go and tell this people: Be ever hearing, but never understanding; be ever seeing, but never perceiving."
>
> Isaiah 6:9, NIV

When the Lord saw that Isaiah was willing to be sent, He gave him an uncomfortable message to share: tell the people that they are blind and deaf. Blindness in ancient times was one of the worst things that could happen to a person. If a person was blinded, unless they had a good family, the only way to support themselves would be through begging. Blindness takes away a person's ability to experience the beauty of the world around them. This message would not curry Isaiah favor in the royal circles, or among his critics. In fact, Isaiah would one day be martyred because he made those in power uncomfortable. The Lord said to Isaiah in Hebrew *shama, shama* or "you hear, you hear." This word means to physically hear and is used twice for emphasis, "but you do not *biyn*," which means to understand. This Hebrew word means to understand beyond the physical senses. He goes on to say *ra'ah, ra'ahor* or "you see, you see, (also used twice for emphasis) but you do not *yadah*." The Hebrew *yadah* means to know or perceive. This word is the same word used to discuss the relationship between a husband and wife that results in the conception of a child. It is the deepest type of human intimacy and speaks of a deep knowing between two people that makes the two become one. To put it plainly, the Lord said there is nothing physically wrong with your eyes or ears, it is your heart and soul that have become blind and deaf.

Once while we were ministering in a remote village in the mountains of southern Mexico, we were invited by a local pastor to minister to a family who lived high up on the mountain. As we drove up the mountain, a pastor who was accompanying me on the journey began to confess that even though he taught that God healed in church, he secretly doubted that divine healing was real. He knew this was wrong but felt that his doubt and unbelief were controlling his thoughts. I asked him a simple question, "Are you willing to allow the Lord to reveal to you the moment when you first began to doubt?" We prayed together in my truck as we arrived at the end of the road. We got out of the truck and met the local pastor and began the long hike up the mountain to minister to the families. When we arrived, we found that no one in the family really understood Spanish. In many rural regions of the Mexican state of Oaxaca, there are small clusters of people groups in the mountains who live isolated lives and speak their own tribal languages that predate the Spanish language in Mexico. The wife led us into the room to pray for her husband. He was a short and frail indigenous man who the family said was in his 90s. He was laying in his bed in the corner staring blankly into space. Because of the language barrier, we did not know his condition or what he needed prayer for. He was very sick looking and was almost unresponsive to our presence in the room. Suddenly, however, as we prayed for him, he sat up and began looking around the room. He then got out of bed and began to get dressed. His wife screamed and began to cry as her husband greeted us all and walked outside his house. The family was chattering excitedly in the local dialect while the grandmother and some of the other women wept. We knew something significant had just happened but did not understand. Finally, someone walked into the room who could speak Spanish. He explained that the man had gone blind 30 years ago and had become very sick six months ago and had been bedridden. The family fully expected that he would not recover and they were preparing for him to pass away. However, as we prayed for him, God healed his vision and his body at the same time. For that reason, he got out of bed and went outside to see his beloved mountains that he had not seen in 30 years. The pastor who accompanied me began to weep as the Lord healed the wounds that had caused doubt and unbelief to become a stronghold in his life. There on the mountain two pairs of blinded eyes were opened by Jesus that day, one physically blind, and the other spiritually blind.

Sometimes we fail to see what Jesus is doing because our hearts have become blinded by religion. In Luke 4:16-30, Jesus inaugurated

His ministry in His hometown by quoting the prophet Isaiah. Jesus read this messianic prophesy as a bold declaration of His purpose and mission among them, even going so far as to say that this Scripture has been fulfilled in front of them. They were amazed at His words and could discern the anointing upon Him, but suddenly they stepped out of the true reality and began to focus on what was in front of their eyes. The problem was that they knew Jesus well but could not discern who He really was. The river of the Spirit flows to the humble; the healing power of Jesus flows to those who recognize how great their need is of Him. People often ask me why I have seen more miracles done in developing countries where few people are Christians. In my humble opinion, the reason is because the people have not been inoculated by religion. When someone receives a shot, they are usually receiving a dead or weakened version of the real virus. Many people today are blind and deaf like the people of Nazareth to the presence of Jesus because they have only encountered religion, which is a form of godliness devoid of power. This blinded them and stopped them from truly knowing who Jesus was, not just according to the physical, but by the Spirit. They could not discern the anointing or the mission of Jesus even though He plainly revealed Himself to them. They could not see what he desired to do among them.

In our lives it can sometimes be very easy to miss what Jesus is doing because we cannot see beyond what our eyes can see and ears can hear. In the book of Luke, we find Jesus walking on the road to Emmaus with His followers after He had already been resurrected. He approached them and began to walk with them, striking up a conversation:

> But their eyes were kept from recognizing him. And he said to them, "What is this conversation that you are holding with each other as you walk?"
>
> Luke 24:16-17

Sometimes, like those disciples we fail to discern what He is actually doing. We need Jesus to open our eyes and allow us to truly see what He is doing around us. The Lord illustrated the need for healing from spiritual blindness to me through a miracle I saw Him do in 2015 while on a crusade in the town of Miguel Aleman, Mexico. I had a word of knowledge that the Lord wanted to heal someone who had a problem with their eyes. An elderly man came to the front. He told me that he wanted healing because he was blind in one eye and did not have good vision in the other eye. I looked at his eye, it was white with a big scar across the front. I laid hands on his eyes and began to pray. As I prayed, I heard the Lord speak to me.

He asked me, "Which is easier for Me to do, heal the eye of a blind man or open the eyes of a blinded nation?"

I was surprised by this, and was not sure how to respond. "I guess it is the same for you," I replied.

I heard the Lord say, "You will see both."

I took my hands off of his eyes and watched as a big smile spread across his face. "I can see!" the old man shouted! Everyone erupted in cheers giving glory to God. The old man reached out and took my hand, asking if I could please pray for his deaf wife. He went back to his seat to bring her up. She was completely deaf in one ear and partially deaf in the other. I laid hands on her ears and again heard the Lord speak.

He asked me, "Which is easier for Me to do, open the ear of a deaf woman or open the ears of a deaf nation?"

"It is the same for you," I again replied.

"Yes," the Lord said, "You will see both in this nation."

I took my hands off of her ears and snapped my finger by her deaf ear while she covered her better ear. A look of surprise came across her face as she said, "I can hear!" We continued testing her ear and saw that God had restored her hearing.

Sometimes we think that one type of miracle is more difficult than another. I used to think in the past that for God to heal cancer was much harder than for Him to heal a headache. It was harder for the Lord to heal blind eyes than for Him to heal a sore knee. It was much easier for Him to do any physical miracle than to bring a sweeping revival that results in thousands being saved. In that moment, I realized that I needed to change my way of thinking. No miracle is too hard for God, because He truly has no limitations. The greatest limitation in our ability to truly believe is found in our ability to discern what He is doing.

After sharing the strategy the Lord had given us with our team, we gave all of our students the option to return home if they felt they needed to leave. They all decided to stay. We began to press into the presence of the Lord and God began to do miracles like we had never seen before.

One of our students was a man named Howard. Howard was very open with us about the fact that he was here at the school as a last resort. After a long career in the military and law enforcement he was both physically and emotionally destroyed. The physical pain in his body and the emotional torment of post-traumatic stress had caused him to fall into an alcohol addiction. He contacted our school asking to come and we felt strongly that he should. He arrived and was immediately ready to leave. The spiritually charged atmosphere of worship, prayer and the move of the Holy Spirit was more than he thought he could handle.

One morning, other students who shared the room with Howard tried to wake him up but could not. The staff of the school became very worried that he was sick or dead. A nurse practitioner on our staff came and found that his vitals were normal except for elevated blood pressure which he had been on medicine for. For just a moment he awoke and said the words "Jesus." Don tried to wake up Howard as well but could not. Don and the staff needed to make a decision on whether to take Howard to the hospital or not. Don felt peace that everything would be fine so he decided to leave Howard and start the classes that morning. Norma, the nurse, stayed with him for about 45 minutes until he regained consciousness. He then came to the classroom to share what had happened to him with a huge smile on his face. When he went to bed the night before, Jesus came to meet him. He left his body behind and for at least 9 hours walked with Jesus in heaven. He said that he could see his body lying there in the bed but knew he was with Jesus. Jesus took him back to every painful and traumatic memory he had ever experienced and healed him completely. When Jesus sent him back into his body he awoke as a completely different man, healed and full of joy. The following night he slept through the night without night terrors for the first time in decades. Upon returning to his home, his relationships with his wife and family (who he had been estranged from for a number of years) were completely restored. This couple is now serving Jesus as part of our mission school leadership team!

In the same school of missions, a young lady named Joanna joined us as a student from Ciudad Juarez, Mexico. Her church did not believe that all the gifts of the Holy Spirit were for today and those that were for today were only available to an elite group of ministers, not for everyone. They made it clear to her that they did not want her coming to our school. In her church everything was tightly controlled and people were not encouraged to go deeper with the Lord. Her pastors tried to discourage her from coming to our school but she still felt she needed to come. From day one, she was very suspicious of everything that was happening. The moving of the Holy Spirit was unlike anything she had ever seen. But she was so afraid of being deceived that she distanced herself from everyone.

When the Lord would be moving in the class times or during the services, she would step aside and closely observe everything that was going on. She made it clear that she trusted no one, and refused to allow anyone to minister to her. However, the root of her fear was based in the hurt and rejection she had experienced throughout her life. She desperately wanted to have her heart healed but did not know how to receive the healing of the Lord. With everything in her, she truly desired to encounter God and flow in His Spirit. Her desire was to encounter God in a real and tangible way that was undeniably Him.

One day, one of our staff was teaching on the love of the Father. This simple word impacted her deeply. She walked out of class with the realization that because of her wounded heart she did not know how to love. Nor did she know how to receive the love of others or the love of God. She was shocked; she had been a Christian for a long time but realized in that moment that she felt no love for anyone else. As she stood up on the rooftop terrace of our school, she felt compelled to ask others to pray for her, something she had not done since she arrived. She went down to the church just as worship was starting. She gathered a few of the staff and students around her and began to confess to them that she did not know how to love or be loved and that she needed prayer. As they began to pray for her, she wept and felt fire go into her body. She suddenly began to feel the love of the people who were praying for her and felt the love of the heavenly Father for the first time in her life. As they began to minister to her, her hands were suddenly filled with a fragrant oil. The women around her did not know what it was so they grabbed towels and began to wipe it away, but as soon as they did, more oil began to flow until it was dripping down her arms and onto the floor. She looked down at this sovereign manifestation of the Holy Spirit's anointing amazed. She reached out her hands and began to anoint the other students with this same oil. Her life was changed from that night onward.

These powerful miracles that the Lord did energized our churches and inspired our teams to press on preaching the gospel with boldness. Our churches cooperated with other ministries to begin helping families who had lost their income because of the factories that had shut down due to Covid. It was incredible to see the body of Christ in action with even the newest of believers taking food and a Bible to their unsaved neighbors. It was an incredible time of mobilization for the harvest. We did not know that all of this was simply preparation for what was about to happen in just a few months.

Is there any area in your life that has caused you to become spiritually blind or deaf? Have you been blinded by fear? Doubt? Deafened by unbelief? Is there anything in your life that obstructs you from clearly hearing the will of God for yourself or the people around you? If the answer is yes, I would like to invite you to pray with me and ask the Lord to heal the eyes and ears of your spirit and enable you to discern and know what He is doing around you.

I invite you to lay hands on your eyes and simply say: "Lord Jesus, forgive me for being blind to what you desire to do in my life. Forgive me for my sin that has grieved your Spirit and my unbelief that has quenched the move of the Spirit in my life. Open my eyes Lord, so that I can truly begin to see you moving in every situation of my life. Show me how to see what you are doing and obey with my whole heart."

Now lay hands on your ears and say: "Lord Jesus, touch me with your fire, so that I can truly begin to hear the desires of your heart. Forgive me for being so busy and distracted that I've failed to press in and hear your heartbeat. Lord, give me your heart for the lost and the broken. Give me the heart of a worshipper. Open my ears to hear what you are saying, and give me the courage to obey everything you will ask me to do.

In Jesus name, Amen."

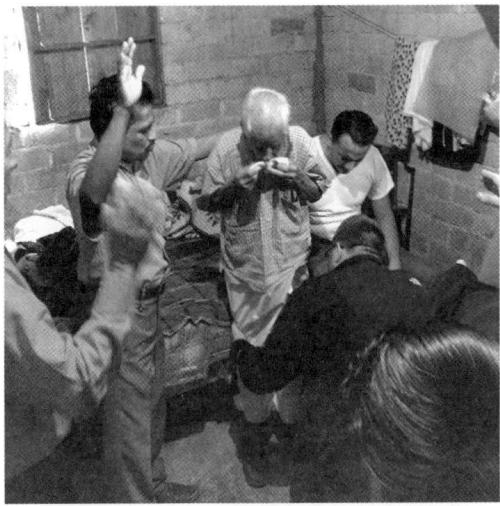

As we prayed for this very sick, elderly blind man, he suddenly sat up and began to look around. He then stood up and began to walk around as we prayed for him.

After receiving healing, the old man stood in his doorway for a long time gazing with tears in his eyes at the beauty of the mountain range outside his door.

The next day, the old man who just a day before, had been too sick to get out of bed, walked down the mountain and joined us for church.

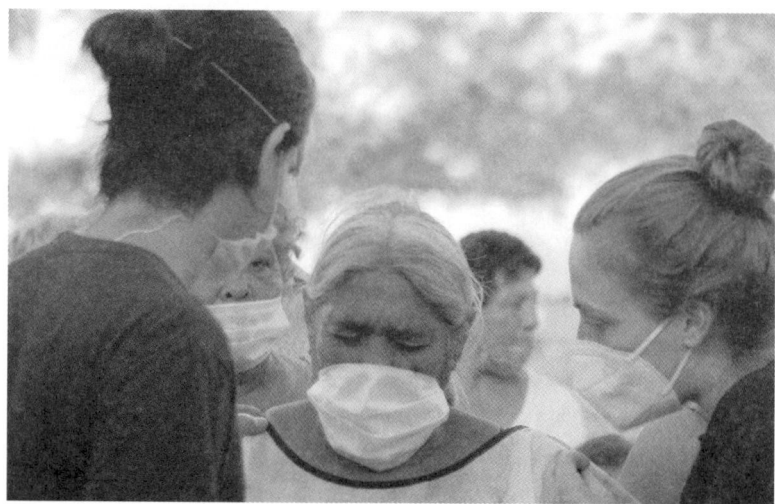

Kaleo Missionaries, Pablo and Alana, ministering at one of our mobile feeding centers.

Seeing and Perceiving

During the pandemic, we estimate we were able to help provide food for around 15,000 at risk families.

CHAPTER 17

THE NEW NORMAL

Once Olivia and I were in the West African nation of Sierra Leone with a team. We had seen God do many powerful miracles during that time. At the end of the trip, we were waiting for a ferry to the island where the airport was, right outside of the capital of Free Town. As we waited for the boat in a small restaurant, a woman came to our table begging for money. She handed us a card in English that said she was mute and deaf and had been that way from birth. We motioned to her with our hands that we wanted to pray for her, she nodded in agreement and closed her eyes as we laid hands on her ears. We began to pray, and suddenly her eyes popped open in shock. She began to wave her hands excitedly at another man across the room. He came over and explained that he was her brother. He began to communicate with her using sign language and interpreted for us. She had never heard before but as we prayed, she suddenly began to hear what we were saying. Even though she did not understand us, she could hear us speaking clearly—something she had never experienced before in her whole life. With her brother interpreting she told us that she now believed in Jesus. She was even able to repeat after us and say the name Jesus out loud, something that she had never been able to do! Tears streamed down her face as she heard for the first time the sound of her baby babbling. Her brother told us that he was amazed because she had never heard before and that he would commit to teach her how to speak their language.

To me this was one of the most powerful illustrations I had ever seen of what new life in the Kingdom looks like for each of us when we encounter the Lord. Just like this woman who had never experienced what it was like to physically hear, you and I were apart from Him and unable to comprehend the reality of His Kingdom. She was deaf physically but we were spiritually deaf and blind. When we become born again and are touched by His fire in the baptism of the Holy Spirit, our world changes as our eyes and ears open to the reality of heaven. Just like this deaf woman, we don't know how to operate in this new reality and need someone to take us by the hand and guide us.

I love to think about the back stories of the miracles that happened in the Bible and to put myself in the shoes of the people encountering Jesus. Take for example, the man who Jesus healed who was born blind. Can you imagine the shock to his mind and body when that sense that had been dead all his life was suddenly healed and he could see? That one moment changed everything he thought he knew about the world he lived in. That one touch from Jesus opened a new world for him that he only knew from other's descriptions.

Think about the demonized man, who had probably lived most of his life in a swirl of demonic insanity. He had so lost who he truly was that he was completely incapable of functioning anymore. Can you imagine what it was like for him when Jesus cast out the legion of tormenting spirits? The sudden return to sanity must have left him breathless. Can you imagine what the transition must have even like for him to begin to live as a sane man among his people again? In much the same way, you and I must learn what it means to live in the new reality of the Kingdom when God opens our eyes and ears to what

He is truly doing around us. The walk of faith involves stepping into a completely different dimension far outside the limited confines of our earthly reality. Jesus told His disciples:

> If you love me, you will keep my commandments. And I will ask the Father, and he will give you another Helper, to be with you forever, even the Spirit of truth, whom the world cannot receive, because it neither sees him nor knows him. You know him, for he dwells with you and will be in you. I will not leave you as orphans; I will come to you. Yet a little while and the world will see me no more, but you will see me. Because I live, you also will live. In that day you will know that I am in my Father, and you in me, and I in you.
>
> John 14:15-20

Part of learning to walk in the reality of the Kingdom involves learning to obey what Jesus commands. Many people mistakenly think that Jesus did away with the law; that is simply not true. Jesus said,

> Do not think that I have come to abolish the Law or the Prophets; I have not come to abolish them but to fulfill them.
>
> Matthew 5:17

Far from His death doing away with commandments of the Lord, His death on our behalf actually made a way for the law to be fulfilled. He knew that we would not have the power to obey His commandments on our own, so He promised to send us the Helper, who is the Holy Spirit. He comes to guide us and help us to live by faith in this new reality and to be victorious in our battle against sin, self, and satan because of His blood shed on our behalf. Just like the deaf woman needed her brother to teach her a new language, we need the Holy Spirit of God to teach us how to hear and obey the commands of Jesus and how to live by faith. The Holy Spirit within us empowers us in a way that the external motivator of the law never could. The motivation of the law is punishment while the motivation of grace is love. The Holy Spirit dwelling in us gives us the ability to have constant contact with our heavenly Father. For that reason, Jesus said that He would not leave us like orphans but would send His Spirit.

And that even though the world would not see Jesus, His disciples would see Him and know Him. The world cannot comprehend what it means to follow a God it cannot see, for that reason it is easier for most people to worship idols. Faith in Jesus however is not blind, nor ignorant; it is actually the greatest form of sight available to us. It is a knowing of the Father by the Spirit that surpasses any earthly form of hearing or sight. Faith means much more than simply asking Jesus into our heart. It involves truly disappearing into Christ Himself, to the point where our own life is completely intermingled into the life of our Savior. Yet despite this heavenly reality, our faith is imperfect and we don't always see as we should. Like a baby learning to walk, we stumble and fall many times. But despite our imperfections, the Holy Spirit takes our hand and leads us deeper into Christ Himself. The apostle Paul said,

> I am crucified with Christ: nevertheless, I live; yet not I, but Christ liveth in me: and the life which I now live in the flesh I live by the faith of the Son of God, who loved me, and gave himself for me.
>
> Galatians 2:20, KJV

I believe that the King James version most accurately captures the intent of Paul's words when it says that this life Paul now lives in the flesh he lives "by the faith of the Son of God." I believe Paul was saying that the supernatural life he lived here on earth was not based on his own faith or ability to believe, but instead was a sovereign work of the Lord's grace. It was indeed the faith of Christ Himself working through Paul to complete the mission that Paul had been assigned to do. Of course this supernatural faith still requires us to position ourselves for His supernatural miracle-working grace to be able to manifest in our lives.

After my wife and I had been married for a number of years, we were believing we would have a baby but we became very concerned since we were not getting pregnant. For several years we were praying and believing but had not received the answer to our prayers. One day as my wife and I were praying, I felt faith rise up in my heart and suddenly out of my mouth I heard myself say that I would commit to fast every day until she was pregnant. Honestly, I was shocked at my own words. I could not believe I had committed to do this. Thoughts ran through my mind, what if this takes years, how do I fulfill my commitment to the Lord? I heard the Holy Spirit speak to me in that moment saying, "My strength is made perfect in your weakness." Taking ahold of the promises of Jesus requires us to step out with a supernatural faith. This supernatural gift of faith pushes us to a level of commitment far beyond our natural abilities. I began fasting two meals a day, not knowing how long this would take. We declared the word daily over our family. Just a little under a month later, my wife and I discovered we were pregnant with our first born whom we named Caleb. This precious baby was a fulfillment of the promise of the Lord to us. We live in a microwave society and oftentimes expect instant results. Faith requires a commitment from us to stand on His promises even in the midst of the battle. The Apostle Paul said,

> ...and having done all, to stand firm. Stand therefore...
>
> Ephesians 6:13-14

What does it mean to stand firm? It simply means that we must do everything He tells us and leave the results up to Him. In this respect, walking by faith often means that we do a natural thing (lay hands on the sick, declare the word, pray, worship etc.) led and supernaturally empowered by His Holy Spirit. This is the intersection between our faith and our works. As the book of James says:

> ...faith by itself, if it does not have works, is dead.
>
> James 2:17

The word of God compels us to put what we believe by faith into action through acts of obedience to His Spirit and His word. This is the substance of our faith, to believe God enough to step out and be willing to seem like a fool in the eyes of the world. It is this kind of radical faith that enables us to stand when everything around us seems to contradict the promises of the Lord. This is the kind of faith that pleases God and enables us to grow in the favor of the Lord. Favor is something that we grow in as we consistently choose to walk by faith.

The Bible says that Jesus Himself also walked through this process as He was preparing for His public ministry.

> And Jesus increased in wisdom and in stature and in favor with God and man.
>
> Luke 2:52

Being born again can happen in an instant, but growing in Christ takes constancy and commitment to walk as a disciple of Christ. The favor of the Lord is something we must grow in through consistently seeking to obey His will. In a similar way, the favor of man is built through consistently allowing the character of Christ to be lived out through us in our communities. This is how we can truly shine as a light for Jesus in dark places. Once we know Jesus, our lives are forever different; we literally become something new that is not of this world. This naturally causes other people to take notice of what has happened in our lives. Not only do we begin to see things differently, but those around us, even non-believers, also begin to see something different in us.

One time I was taking a group of Americans who were visiting us in Reynosa to the immigration office to get their visas. While I was waiting for them to fill out their paperwork I stepped outside the office to take a phone call. After I finished the call, a man came walking up to me and started the conversation by saying that he had been watching me. I took a step back and braced myself for what he might say. He saw my defensive posture and immediately began to clarify that he worked in the office and that he had seen me come into that office many times before. He said that the first time he saw me he was amazed because there was a shining light around my face. Then when I came back again with a team, he saw the same light around us all. He was perplexed and had never seen anything like this before. Several times over the years he tried to start a conversation with me, but the office was always too busy for him to be able come and ask me why I was shining. Finally that night he saw his chance to come and talk to me while I was outside the office by myself. I began to share the gospel with him and shared that the reason my face was shining was because of the presence of Jesus in my life. As you disappear into Jesus, the people around you should begin to see you less and less and see Him shining brighter and brighter.

The New Normal

Once while on an outreach with Iris Ministries in Mozambique, my wife and I along with a team from the Harvest School were in a remote village. Our team arrived in the village and set up our tents where we would be sleeping. After setting up, most of the team went off to share the gospel and minister house-to-house. Olivia and I stayed back with some of the Mozambican pastors to watch the tents, making sure nothing was stolen. After a few hours a man dressed from another religion came and wanted to speak with us. He explained that his sister had severely burned her leg and it had become infected. She was at his home with a high fever. The family was very concerned about her and was afraid that she would die. They tried to find a solution but the medical facilities were very far and they did not have the money. That night, however, as everyone slept, the brother had a dream about a man dressed in white. This man introduced Himself as Jesus and told him not to be afraid. Jesus told the man in the dream that His servants were coming to the village the next day and that they would heal his sister and tell him how to follow God. The man awoke from the dream amazed at what he had just heard. The next morning, he set off to come and find us. He found us setting up our tents. We agreed along with some of the Mozambican pastors to go and pray for his sister. When we arrived, we found the women in bed burning up from a high fever. Her wound was poorly bandaged with dirty rags. We began to pray as Olivia began to disinfect and dress the wound with a fresh bandage. As we prayed, her fever broke. We shared the gospel with the entire family. The brother who had had the dream of Jesus spoke for the family as the head of the house that they would choose to follow Jesus. They brought out all of their witchcraft items and we burned them in front of the house as a public declaration to their neighbors that they would now follow Jesus. After making this decision and burning their witchcraft items, the woman was healed supernaturally and began to walk around completely healed.

Everything about the Christian life is miraculous. Apart from the Holy Spirit, the walk of faith is impossible. In order to walk the walk of faith we must recognize that our lives are no longer our own. We are now in Christ. This kind of daily surrender enables us to follow Jesus and obey what He tells us to do each day. As we follow Him, the same miracles that followed Jesus everywhere will also follow us.

Olivia and I welcoming our son Caleb into the world!

The New Normal

Preaching in an open-air campaign in western Kenya.

CHAPTER 18

THE FIRE, THE PLAGUE AND THE FLOOD

In 2019, my wife and I found out that we were pregnant with our second child. We were both thrilled and ecstatic about this precious blessing of the Lord. We had just told our families and were preparing to announce it to everyone when suddenly my wife began to bleed. I rushed her to the doctor and the doctor informed us that we had lost the pregnancy. It was a brutal shock. We had done everything we could, we had prayed, I had fasted, but sadly we lost the baby. Neither of us had ever experienced such an intense sadness. This was on a Saturday and I was scheduled to preach on Sunday at our church in Reynosa. I arranged for someone to help Olivia and I left the house to preach. I arrived at the church, and during worship I laid on the ground weeping.

"I have nothing to give today, I cannot even organize my thoughts...how can I possibly preach?" I said to the Lord.

Suddenly, I heard the Lord ask me a question,

"What do you want from me, my son?"

I was filled in that moment with an intense mixture of anger and joy. Anger at the enemy for what had been stolen from us and joy because I knew that the Lord was about to turn this entire situation around for His glory.

"I want revival!" I said. "Our people need your presence to be poured out!"

"Stand up and release that revival," The Lord replied.

I got up and took the microphone for the transition from worship into preaching. I tried to speak but the words would not come out, so I just began to speak in tongues. No one in the church except our missionaries and pastors knew what had happened the day before. But much to my surprise, as I began to sing in tongues people throughout the room began to weep under the power of God. Even some of our most reserved church members began to spontaneously come to the altar and cry out to God. A group of children from our church came to receive prayer. As I began to lay hands on them, I was suddenly taken into a vision. In the vision, I saw a little blond haired boy dancing and laughing with Jesus. The little boy waved at me and then disappeared. I knew that this was my son. After I came out of the vision, I saw that these same group of children around me were now laid out on the floor weeping and speaking in tongues. This service went on for many more hours as both children and adults wept, laughed, and worshipped Jesus together.

I remain firmly convinced that God is good because I know His character. I also know the craftiness of our enemy and I know that sometimes things happen in our lives that we cannot comprehend. It is in those moments more than ever that we must press into the goodness of our heavenly Father. This should put a holy anger inside of us to come against the enemy harder than ever before and by faith begin to ask bigger things from God than we have had the courage to ask before. Jesus said:

> From the days of John the Baptist until now the kingdom of heaven has suffered violence, and the violent take it by force.
>
> Matthew 11:12

The Christian life is not meant to be a passive affair. God does not desire religious, emotionless robotic obedience. He is looking for people who passionately pursue God with everything they have, and who confront the violent attacks of the enemy with sword of the Spirit, the power of His word and a supernatural faith. This is the kind of faith that God calls us to have in the middle of adversity, faith that does not wallow in defeat but takes the fight to the enemy. In the following months, the Lord continued to heal and restore us as the presence of the Lord continued to break out in our church meetings in greater measure.

As few months later, my wife and I found out that we were pregnant again. Our excitement was mixed with sadness and concern. We continued to stand on the Word and believe that everything would go well. During that time, I made a trip to visit our Kaleo Bible College and churches in Kenya. One night while I was in the church, I got a call from my wife. She was sobbing as she explained that she had been to the doctor and the doctor told her that there was a serious problem and that she would most likely lose this baby as well. I could feel the fear trying to grab hold of my heart. I was speechless for a few minutes but after a little while I spoke up and told my wife that I would try to get another flight and come home.

"No," she replied, "you need to finish your mission there in Kenya."

"No, I need to be there with you, so I can pray and fast," I replied.

"You can do that there. There's nothing that you can do here that you cannot do there," she said.

As we prayed and said goodbye I felt a horrible fear, so tangible and real that it felt like a cold hand grasping my heart. I began to pray in tongues, and for the next week I dedicated myself to prayer and fasting. Our precious church family and team in Reynosa took care of Olivia and our son while I was away. During that time when I was not teaching or preaching, I was praying via video call with dear friends who had agreed to intercede for the life of this baby. I will always be grateful for dear friends like Angie, Tineke, Peter, Victor, Pepe, Kelly, Don and Jackie just to name a few who were available to pray with me both in person and on the phone for hours at a time as we prayed in the Spirit. A week later while I was sitting in an airport in Rwanda, I got a call from my wife that she had just left the doctor's office and the doctor was amazed to discover that everything was completely normal! Our daughter, Sarah, was born some months later at the very beginning of 2020.

At the beginning of 2020, our ministry did a 40 day fast involving our missionaries and churches around the world. I felt the Lord saying we needed to prepare ourselves for the next wave of the Holy Spirit that the Lord wanted to bring! As we pressed into the Lord's presence, I heard the Lord say, "Prepare yourselves for a move of my Spirit but be prepared because it will look different than you think it will." Sometimes revival does not come in the nice neat package we expect it to. Sometimes the stage prepared for a move of God is one of worldly chaos and destruction. The greatest opportunities to shine occur during times when the world around us is in crisis. The church has always grown the most during chaotic times, but only when people truly see the crises around them with the eyes of the Holy Spirit. I am not advocating a religious form of preaching that spews judgment and condemnation every time there is a disaster nor am I saying that every disaster is an "act of God."

The reality is that we live in a fallen world marred by the effects of sin. I have served much of my life in war-torn countries and have seen firsthand the horrible things mankind is capable of doing to each other. I have also seen the devastation caused by natural disasters that shake people to their core. Despite this, I have learned that the key to remaining joyful and optimistic is to constantly ask God to allow me to see through His eyes. Walking by faith means allowing God to open our eyes in order to see the opportunities to show the love of God to people who are experiencing crisis. What the world sees as a chaotic storm, a man or women filled with faith sees as an opportunity for a miracle.

In July of 2020 in the middle of the pandemic, hurricane Hanna struck the region of Mexico where we live. This hurricane remained over our city for hours and poured out floods of rain water. The canals and rivers overflowed their banks and much of the city was engulfed in flash floods. Thousands of people's homes were completely underwater; the devastation was tremendous. After the brunt of the hurricane had passed over us, I told my wife that I needed to go check on our people. Cell phone reception was down so I set out in my truck to check on the people from our churches. After several hours navigating flooded streets, I arrived at our base in Reynosa. The bottom level was flooded. Our sound system and chairs were floating. I was shocked. This area was so much higher than anywhere else in the neighborhood that we never thought the waters would get in. We began cleaning the building out and trying to see what we could salvage. In that moment I was a bit lost in self-pity, thinking about how much money we had lost with our sound system and other things that were destroyed. Suddenly, one of our neighbors arrived asking us to come help her father-in-law who was struggling to get out of their house.

I heard the Holy Spirit speak to me and say,

"Love your neighbors and do not miss what I am going to do in the middle of this."

This statement brought me back to reality. I quietly repented for my selfish attitude and went out with some of our missionaries to help the people who lived around our base and saw how much worse their houses had flooded than ours. We opened up our churches as emergency shelters and began helping get families out of their homes. As our churches and team jumped into action to begin to help our community, it became obvious how bad the situation was. Many churches joined together to make food and provide fresh water to people who had been affected. Our team went to take food into a community near the lake where the community had been flooded with 8-to-10-foot flood waters. We were stopped by soldiers who informed us that we could not go in without a boat. We offered to help them if they had a boat, and they informed us that they did not have the boats they needed to help people either.

"If I can find a boat, will you all help me take this food to the people?" I asked.

They looked a little bit puzzled and amused but replied that yes, they would help us if I could find a boat. I called a friend who was a businessman in the community and asked if we could borrow a boat from him. He replied that we could, however, his boat was very old and he did not know if it would work or not. We decided to take the chance and brought the boat out. After about 40 minutes, however, we realized that the boat had a major leak. Unfortunately, we had to get out and push the boat back to shallow water. We spent hours fighting the fast-moving currents, up to our shoulders in filthy flood waters. That night I returned to my home exhausted and feeling completely defeated. I could not shake the feeling that we needed a boat in order to better help the people. The next morning, I spoke to my wife and shared that I felt we needed to get a boat to help with the disaster relief. We began to look and found one in Texas to buy. We negotiated a good price but did not have the money to buy it. So, I left to buy the boat by faith and before I reached the owners' home, someone had sent us the money we needed to make the purchase. We took the boat out into the water and began to help people get out of their houses and take food to the people who had chosen to stay on their roofs.

We heard about a village outside of Reynosa that had been flooded and that no one had been in or out for the past three days. I felt immediately from the Holy Spirit that we were to go there. This small village had a population of around 200 but we could not find it on any maps. We went to the nearest town we could find on the map. There we found hundreds of people from the surrounding villages who had come to escape the flooding. They were mad almost to the point of rioting because no one from the government had been to check on them or help them yet. We arrived pulling our boat and I went into the crowd asking if anyone knew where the village of Los Altos was. A woman came forward saying that her daughter was from there and could help us. She called over a lady whose name was Sandra. Sandra agreed to take us there. We arrived outside of the village and found that the river had completely covered the road.

We put our boat down into the water and by God's grace were able to navigate the fast-moving waters. People heard us coming and came out of their houses to come and receive the food and supplies. We began to preach the gospel to the people, and many prayed with us to accept Jesus as their Savior, including Sandra, the lady who had brought us there.

A few days after the flood waters had receded, we went back to follow up with the people who had received the Lord and to plant house groups. In one of the groups, Sandra stood up to testify. She said to them, "You all know me, and you know that all of my life I have worshiped the saint of death. After I received Jesus on the bridge, I heard the voice of God speak to me and tell me to return to my house and destroy every altar and idol that I owned. Last night I destroyed many idols worth lots of money. I want to tell you that today I am declaring that I trust in Jesus Christ alone." The people were amazed, Sandra had been dedicated to the saint of death since she was a child. Word spread through the villages about Jesus' power over the spirit of death. During this time, we planted multiple new house groups and churches.

During the flooding we gave out as much food as we could, but no matter how fast we would give it away there was always enough. During the time of the flooding and in the months that followed, our team was able to distribute 11 semitrailers filled with food into the communities that were hardest hit by the floods and Covid shutdowns. By God's grace, we fed approximately 10,000 families during that time.

A few months later in November 2020, we hosted a gathering of our leaders and churches. This time of great difficulty had birthed a hunger in our ministry for a greater measure of the Lord's presence among us. A pastor from Tulsa, Oklahoma named John Peña came to minister. There were amazing supernatural manifestations of the Holy Spirit during this time. During one of the ministry times, he called up anyone in our church who had problems with their teeth. Several people came forward. We prayed for them all, two of the ladies felt something happening in their mouths. They ran into the bathroom to check their teeth in the mirror. Both came out amazed because their teeth that had once been open cavities were now filled with a hard metal substance. One of the women was a pastor in our church had two cavities filled with a golden-colored metal. The other lady who was a member of our church had two teeth filled with a silver-colored metal. Both testified that they had not received any dental work on those teeth and that these metal fillings had not been there before but had been placed there by the Holy Spirit. Another lady who had been diagnosed with a cancerous tumor came back the next day with a report from the doctor that her tumor had disappeared. As I sat there watching these amazing miracles with tears in my eyes, thinking of all that had happened during this year, the Lord spoke to me and reminded me of the word I had received at the beginning of the year. It truly was a year of restoring our vision.

Our Kaleo International Bible Institute in western Kenya. Here pictured are a number of our Kaleo church leaders and pastors from Kenya, Uganda and South Sudan.

The Maasai are a nomadic, cattle herding tribe in Kenya.

Welcoming our miracle baby, Sarah, into the world!

Devastation from hurricane Hanna.

The Fire, the Plague and the Flood

Going by boat to access difficult to reach areas affected by flooding.

Preaching the gospel as people receive food and provisions.

Our neighbors who lost many of their food supplies and possessions in the flood receiving food.

Our team taking emergency supplies by boat to a village that had been stranded for 3 days because the canals had overflown their banks and flooded the only roads in.

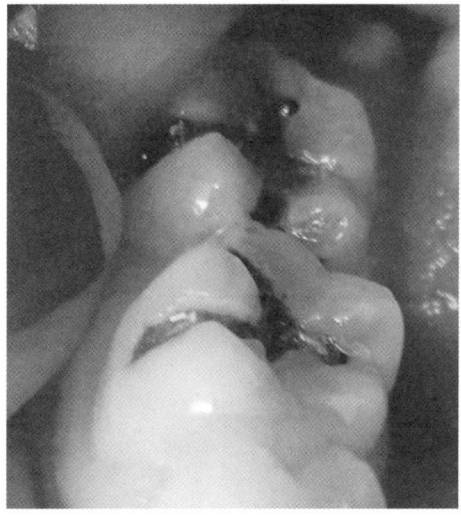

One of our leaders received 2 silver fillings when pastor John Peña prayed for her.

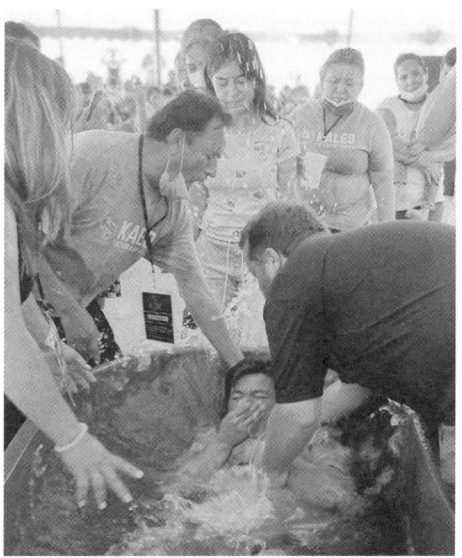

"Do you not know that all of us who have been baptized into Christ Jesus were baptized into his death? We were buried therefore with him by baptism into death, in order that, just as Christ was raised from the dead by the glory of the Father, we too might walk in newness of life." - Romans 6:3-4

CHAPTER 19

FOLLOW THE FIRE

Jaime had been a drug dealer and drug addict for most of his life. His addiction was destroying his health and peace of mind, as well as his family. In the small town where he lived in Mexico, Jaime was well known as the person who could keep you supplied with drugs. One day, however, Jaime saw a strange sight. He saw what appeared to be a joyful man literally burning with fire, dancing, and jumping down the main street of his small town. He looked around and was amazed that no one seemed to be able to see this burning man skipping, almost floating down the road. Because of his curiosity, he took off running down the street following this joyful fiery being. The burning man led Jaime to what was a large event center, and as suddenly as he had appeared, he disappeared inside. Jaime was truly perplexed. Who was this man? Why did he lead him to this building? A few days later he found out that the building where the man had entered was one of our Kaleo churches. It was a brand-new church that did not even have a sign yet. He came a few days later while we were doing a meeting at the church. He gave his heart to Jesus and the Lord set him free from many demons. The next day he told us that he wanted to publicly acknowledge his faith in Christ and be baptized. I believe that the burning man Jaime saw that day was the Holy Spirit Himself guiding him to a place of deliverance and encounter.

What the Holy Spirit does in us privately is what He then desires to manifest through us publicly to touch the lives of others. We started this book talking about Moses' encounter with the burning bush in the desert. When Moses returned to Egypt, not everyone believed what had happened to him in the wilderness. But when the miracles began to happen even his enemies had to take note. The difference in his life was unmistakable; the fire had changed him from a slave to a liberator. After leading the Israelites out of Egypt he took them into the desert, where the same fire that Moses had seen in the burning bush was now manifested before an entire nation as a pillar of cloud and fire that led them.

> And the Lord went before them by day in a pillar of cloud to lead them along the way, and by night in a pillar of fire to give them light, that they might travel by day and by night. The pillar of cloud by day and the pillar of fire by night did not depart from before the people.
>
> Exodus 13:21-22

Many people never fulfill their calling from the Lord because they are afraid of the unknown. The reality is that God, in His mercy, does not show us what every step of the journey will be. He normally only illuminates the next step we need to take. This is good for us, because if He did show us everything, most of us would probably never step out in the beginning. Many believers have great dreams of doing big things for God but remain stuck because they refuse to take the simple, non-glamorous steps required to follow the Lord in daily obedience. True radical faith can only be cultivated through daily obedience and pursuit of His presence.

Once a young man came to me asking for advice at a school of ministry where I was speaking. He seemed very concerned because he wanted to hear the Lord telling him what to do next but had not heard any directional word. I simply asked, what was the last direction the Lord had given him? He thought about it, and told me something the Lord had spoken to him several months ago. He tried to change the subject back to his big plans he wanted to do for the Lord. "Did you obey the last word the Lord gave you?" I asked. He thought about it for a moment, puzzled about what something so insignificant had to do with his big plans. I asked him a simple question: "How can God trust you to do great things when you are not willing to obey Him in the small things?" Following the fire means that we must obey even when it's inconvenient. We must press in for more and cultivate a hunger for the Lord that is so passionate it cannot be satisfied by anything other than the Lord's presence.

I have always been amazed how the Lord will order our steps if we allow Him to. When I was in high school I had the opportunity to study Chinese for a few semesters with a retired missionary who had spent many years in Taiwan. I knew that God was calling me as a missionary, but did not feel that that call was for China. However, I felt strongly that taking this course was an important opportunity from the Lord. After the class ended and I graduated from high school, I thought to myself maybe I had wasted my time. A few months later, however, I heard the Lord tell me that I needed to go to China during the Beijing Olympics. I found a mission team who was going there and allowed me to come with them. I ended up with a small team in a large city in the north east of the country. I was desperately trying to remember the little bit of Chinese I had learned during my classes. One day while I was in a shopping mall looking for batteries for my camera, I struck up a conversation with some college students who spoke excellent English. They asked me my name. I replied in Chinese, introducing myself with a name my Chinese teacher had given me years before (little did they know that it was the only phrase I could remember in the moment). The name meant "the prevailing grace of God." This was a common name for Christians in Taiwan but not common at all on the communist mainland. They looked at each other and asked if we could meet again. I said yes.

A few days later we arranged a meeting in a restaurant. As is the custom, we exchanged a few small gifts. One of the young ladies gave us a picture of herself, surprisingly in the background there was a large image of a cross. I asked her if she knew what the cross meant. She replied that Jesus died on the cross. Then she went on to say that she had heard the story of Jesus dying on the cross from a friend in high school but one day her friend disappeared and she never found out the rest of Jesus' story. When she heard my name, she knew I was probably a Christian and was hoping that perhaps I could tell the rest of Jesus' story. I was amazed at how the Lord had ordered each of these small steps to bring me around the world for this moment where I was able to share the gospel with someone who was seeking to find Jesus. After sharing the gospel, the two young ladies gave their lives to the Lord.

Sometimes as we follow the Lord, He tests our hearts by giving us the opportunity to settle. Having to make a choice again to follow where Jesus leads us, enables us to demonstrate our love for God by choosing to put Him first. In the book of 2 Kings, we find the story of God passing the mantle to Elisha. Elisha was called by the Lord in I Kings 19. Elijah, who is a type and shadow of the Holy Spirit in our lives, approached Elisha, who was at that time a successful land owner and farmer, and simply threw his mantle over his shoulders. Elijah had been told by the Lord that Elisha would be his successor, but he knew that he must first be tested before he could receive the heavy weight of a commission from the Lord. Elisha sacrificed his oxen, burned his farm implements, said goodbye to his family, and followed the prophet. Sacrificing his oxen and burning his plow were powerful expressions of his commitment to follow the Lord by eliminating his "plan B." It was a bold move considering Elijah did not really give him any details of what his new job would entail. Even though there was a call on his life, he was not instantly commissioned as a prophet.

Instead, he spent a significant amount of time humbly serving his master. In the Kingdom, true greatness never comes through self-promotion but instead it comes through humble, faithful service. I am sure that Elijah was not an easy person to serve. He was probably a bit grumpy and cantankerous, but this was part of the process of preparation. In 2 Kings 2, however, the time had finally come for Elisha to be commissioned and to receive the mantle. The Lord took Elisha on a final test to see if he had what it takes to follow the fire no matter what.

> Now when the Lord was about to take Elijah up to heaven by a whirlwind, Elijah and Elisha were on their way from Gilgal. And Elijah said to Elisha, "Please stay here, for the Lord has sent me as far as Bethel." But Elisha said, "As the Lord lives, and as you yourself live, I will not leave you." So they went down to Bethel. And the sons of the prophets who were in Bethel came out to Elisha and said to him, "Do you know that today the Lord will take away your master from over you?" And he said, "Yes, I know it; keep quiet."
>
> Elijah said to him, "Elisha, please stay here, for the Lord has sent me to Jericho." But he said, "As the Lord lives, and as you yourself live, I will not leave you." So they came to Jericho. The sons of the prophets who were at Jericho drew near to Elisha and said to him, "Do you know that today the Lord will take away your master from over you?" And he answered, "Yes, I know it; keep quiet."
>
> Then Elijah said to him, "Please stay here, for the Lord has sent me to the Jordan." But he said, "As the Lord lives, and as you yourself live, I will not leave you." So the two of them went on. Fifty men of the sons of the prophets also went and stood at some distance from them, as they both were standing by the Jordan. Then Elijah took his cloak and rolled it up and struck the water, and the water was parted to the one side and to the other, till the two of them could go over on dry ground. When they had crossed, Elijah said to Elisha, "Ask what I shall do for you, before I am taken from you." And Elisha said, "Please let there be a double portion of your spirit on me." And he said, "You have asked a hard thing; yet, if you see me as I am being

taken from you, it shall be so for you, but if you do not see me, it shall not be so." And as they still went on and talked, behold, chariots of fire and horses of fire separated the two of them. And Elijah went up by a whirlwind into heaven. And Elisha saw it and he cried, "My father, my father! The chariots of Israel and its horsemen!" And he saw him no more. Then he took hold of his own clothes and tore them in two pieces. And he took up the cloak of Elijah that had fallen from him and went back and stood on the bank of the Jordan. Then he took the cloak of Elijah that had fallen from him and struck the water, saying, "Where is the Lord, the God of Elijah?" And when he had struck the water, the water was parted to the one side and to the other, and Elisha went over.

2 Kings 2:1:14

Each of the places Elijah led Elisha through carries prophetic significance. The first place was Gilgal, the place where God led the people of Israel who had been born in the desert to renew their covenant with the Lord through circumcision (Joshua 5). Under the new covenant of Christ, the need for circumcision changed from something physical to something spiritual. The Apostle Paul said,

> ...circumcision is a matter of the heart, by the Spirit, not by the letter...
>
> Romans 2:29

God desires to take us through a process in our hearts whereby He reaffirms our covenant with Him and removes from the us the attitudes of our hearts that displease Him. Yet many believers refuse to move beyond that point in their walk with the Lord and allow the Lord to bring them into maturity. Elijah offered for Elisha to stay back in Gilgal, but Elisha knew that if he ever let go of Elijah he might never be able to find him again. He replied, "As the Lord lives, and as you yourself live, I will not leave you."

Elijah then led him to Bethel. Bethel in Hebrew means "the House of God." It is a wonderful thing to be in God's house surrounded by other believers. Sadly however, many believers have become addicted to comfort and seek to make the house nicer while ignoring the call of the Holy Spirit to step outside their comfort zone and serve in the mission field.

Once while I was preaching at a small church in Texas, an older man came up during the prayer time. I had been preaching about hearing the Lord and saying yes to His call to go and preach the gospel to the nations. The man came up to me with tears in his eyes saying that God had spoken a nation to him. He told me the nation. It was a very closed country where Christianity is illegal. I put my hand on his shoulder and began to pray for the Lord to open a door for this man to go to that nation. He suddenly became very nervous and almost shouted with surprise, "No, not me, I think God wants to send you." He said, "I don't want to go there!" I could not help but laugh. At some point in each of our lives we have all been guilty of the same mistake ourselves. Praying for God to do something and send someone when we ourselves are not willing to go. Again, Elisha refused to stay behind but continued to follow Elijah.

The next town they came to was Jericho. In Israel's history in the promise land, Jericho held a special place as the first miraculous victory God had given them over their enemies. It was a place where God had demonstrated His power and opened the door for Israel to begin their conquest of the land God had given them. It was the first major test for Moses' successor, Joshua. As the walls of Jericho fell before the entire nation, faith arose among the new generation who had been born in the desert that their God could truly do anything. Jericho, however, did not represent the culmination of the promise, but the beginning of the conquest.

Once I was invited to preach in a large church in Mexico. I arrived on a Saturday, prepared to share on Sunday. When I met with the pastor, he was very embarrassed to share that they had double booked me with another guest speaker. I did not have a problem with this as I had heard of this well-known healing evangelist before and looked forward to hearing him minister. The Lord spoke to me Sunday morning and told me to pay attention because He wanted me to learn something from this man. The visiting minister got up to speak. He preached for a while and told lots of stories. Almost all of his stories began with, "20 years ago we saw God heal..." or "15 years ago, God did this miracle." I could feel the faith rising in the room and knew that God wanted to heal people. He then asked if anyone needed healing. People raised their hands and he prayed a general prayer and ended the service without laying hands or praying one-on-one with any of them. I was a little surprised at this but could tell the man seemed tired. As I sat there watching, I heard the Lord say,

"My son, don't allow yourself to become complacent by simply standing on the miracles from the past. Do not allow yourself to be content simply memorializing a past move of my Spirit, I am calling you to stay on the cutting edge."

I do not in any way want to judge this man, but I will not ever forget what the Lord spoke to me that day. Since then, I have continued to ask the Lord to not allow me to become complacent in my pursuit of His presence and to keep me hungry to press in for greater miracles.

Again, in Jericho Elisha had the opportunity to stay. But he chose to press on. We have much to learn from the tenacity of Elisha. In each city he was met by groups of men the Bible refers to as the sons of the prophets. In every place they tried to convince him to stay there with them. In much the same way, as we follow the Holy Spirit, we will also encounter people who have chosen to settle. Sometimes they will not be happy about your choice to radically serve God and will try to convince you to settle as well. When I went on the mission field, many well-meaning believers in my life thought it was just a phase. When I got married, I heard comments like, we are so happy for you, now you can settle down and get a real job. I would simply smile and say that I would stay where God had planted me. Then after having children, my wife and I heard the same questions: people asking, "Aren't you going to move back to the USA for your children now?" We just smiled and said that we will follow Jesus and stay where He plants us. Oftentimes, I have seen people who have a call from the Lord get derailed by the well-meaning "sons of the prophets" in their lives and as a result do not take the step from being called to being commissioned.

We see the commission of Elisha at the Jordan river, when Elijah again offers him the chance to stay back. Again, Elisha refuses as he had before. Elijah turned again to Elisha, and I like to imagine at this point the normally serious Elijah was probably smiling with pride that his spiritual son had passed this series of tests. He asks him a question, "What can I do for you?" Elisha replies, "Please let there be a double portion of your spirit on me." I like to think that this request deeply pleased Elijah—the fact that his spiritual son had the courage to ask such a thing.

Oftentimes I have heard it preached that Elisha wanted double the power in order to do double the miracles of Elijah. Although it is true that he did do double the miracles that Elijah had done, I believe there was something more profound that he was asking for. The double portion of an inheritance was the amount that was given to the firstborn son of the household. The firstborn in the Jewish culture carried the additional burden of becoming the head of his family and taking care of his mother and younger siblings. I believe what Elisha was implying was this: he had served Elijah as a servant for quite some time, but his true desire was to continue with Elijah's mission and mantle not as a servant but as a true son. We must never forget as we follow Jesus that our true destiny is not simply greater power, greater miracles or a greater authority. Our true goal should be to carry the nature, image and mantle of our heavenly Father as true sons. Oftentimes the enemy tries to bury our true identity beneath shame and rejection, but when we encounter our Father as He really is, it restores our identity and purpose and empowers us to follow Him into the supernatural realm.

Elijah took his mantle and struck the river. As the waters parted before them, they walked through. As Elijah and Elisha were talking, chariots of fire came and took Elijah away. As he left, his mantle fell back down to earth. The transferring of this mantle was not something that I believe Elijah had the ability to do on his own. That mantle had to come down from heaven. I believe in impartation through the laying on of hands for the activation of spiritual gifts. However, the commissioning of someone who has been called by the Lord has to come from Jesus Himself. After receiving the mantle, Elisha went back to the Jordan river. I can imagine him looking down at this mantle with a burning question... would God really back him up the way He had always backed up Elijah? He cried out, "Where is the Lord, the God of Elijah?" and struck the water. I am sure, to his amazement, the water parted before him and he walked through on dry land. Elisha had crossed the river that day as a servant with a call from God but he came back across the river as a son carrying the mantle of his father to be sent on a mission.

A number of years ago while I was in Pemba, Mozambique, I was laying on the floor during a powerful time of worship. Suddenly, I saw Jesus standing before me and everything else seemed to disappear. He was dressed in plain brown robes, like that of a carpenter. His beard and hair were dark brown and His eyes shone with joy. He extended his hand to me and as I took it, I was suddenly transformed into a young child dressed in a white robe. Jesus threw back His head and began to laugh. He began to run and it was everything I could do to keep up with Him as He ran laughing and dancing through the nations of the world. I saw many groups of dark, shrouded figures cloaked in rags as we ran. As Jesus approached them, He touched them and they suddenly jumped to life. The black rags disappeared and they suddenly were clothed in white. We continued doing this for quite some time, touching those in darkness and seeing them set free until I could see thousands of children dressed in white robes running with Jesus. Suddenly I was taken to another place in the vision. This place was very different from the first. I found myself in the camp of the enemy. I could see ranks of demons arrayed in battle armor lining up in formation. I heard their terrified voices as they called out to one another saying over and over again:

"The King is coming! The sons of God are coming!"

As I looked past the ranks of demons up over the hill, I saw Jesus. He looked very different than I had seen Him before. Before I had seen the fatherly side of Jesus surrounded by His children. This time I saw Him as a warrior king riding on a white horse. His hair was as white as wool, his robe was dipped in blood, and he wore a glorious crown on His head. He held a sword in His hand and His eyes burned with a holy fire. On every side of Him were countless warriors riding white horses, who looked like smaller versions of Himself. I recognized them as the children He had rescued. The sound of their worship, their joy, and their laughter were like a war cry that shook the ground the enemy stood upon. And as suddenly as I had been taken into the vision, I was taken out of it and stood there breathless.

I heard the Lord speak, saying "This is the army I am sending out. An army of sons and daughters dressed in my holiness, carrying my fire, and preaching my gospel commissioned in My name."

Each of us have such a short time on this earth and we each have to decide how we will use the remaining time we have. I would like to invite you today to join this humble carpenter king; to join with His plan for the redemption of the nations. If you are willing to be commissioned, I would like to invite you to pray this prayer with me.

"Lord, I am listening to your voice. I ask you today to show me the next step and how to obey you. Lord, here I am, send me. Where you lead me, I will follow, where you say to go, I will go. I commit from this day forward to lay down my life to follow after you. Here I am Lord, send me! In Jesus name, Amen."

Jaime being baptized just days after following the Holy Spirit to our church!

Crying out for Jesus!

Olivia and I going by boat to preach to small communities on remote islands off the coast of Tamaulipas.

Baliet, South Sudan.

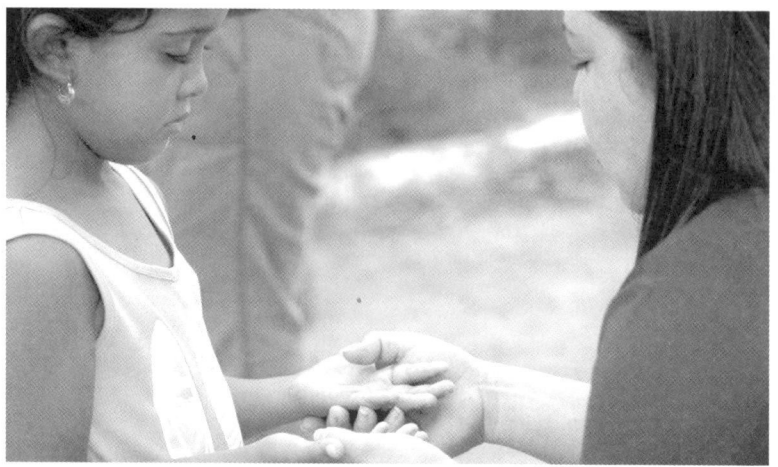

But Jesus said, "Let the little children come to me and do not hinder them, for to such belongs the kingdom of heaven." Matthew 19:14

CONCLUSION

CARRIERS OF THE GLORY

You cannot experience the glory of the Lord and remain the same. Encountering the Lord always brings changes to our hearts. Oftentimes we do not even realize how much we have changed until others point it out. Once when I was preaching at a small church in El Paso, Texas, I noticed a young lady in the congregation looking intently at me. She was dressed in very dark gothic style clothing with black makeup and multiple piercings. During the prayer time I invited people to come to receive prayer. She came forward and told me that she was not a Christian and that she was more into wicca and new age. She had come this night because a Christian friend had invited her, but when she arrived she was amazed to see this white light shining off my face. She said that she had never seen anything like it before and for that reason she decided to stay. The world is looking to encounter the glory of the Lord through you. When

Moses met with God face-to-face on Mount Sinai, his face literally changed because of the glory.

> When Moses came down from Mount Sinai, with the two tablets of the testimony in his hand as he came down from the mountain, Moses did not know that the skin of his face shone because he had been talking with God.
>
> Exodus 34:29

The glory changed him. He looked otherworldly. With his shining, glowing face, he no longer "fit in" among his people. Moses had to cover his face because the world was not ready for the glory that he was carrying. Many years later, Jesus would come and fulfill the standard of the law of Moses. Through His death and resurrection those who believed in Him would have the ability to encounter the same fire and glory that Moses had experienced and carry it into the world. Sometimes, however, like Moses we are tempted to veil our faces in order to fit in better with those around us. Moses had to hide his face, but you and I no longer need to hide from the glory. The apostle Paul said,

> And we all, with unveiled face, beholding the glory of the Lord, are being transformed into the same image from one degree of glory to another. For this comes from the Lord who is the Spirit.
>
> 2 Corinthians 3:18

Just like Moses, we reflect that same glory. The impartation of the glory occurs when we look upon the Lord face-to-face as we worship him. The wording in the Greek for beholding the glory means "to look and reflect as though through a mirror." This means that as we look upon the Lord, He sees His reflection in us. Nothing brings greater pleasure to the heart of a father or mother than to see yourself in your sons and daughters. In the same way, God the Father loves to see His reflection in us. The word glory here in this passage is the word doxa. It is the root word where we get the word doxology. *Doxa* means "splendor or brightness belonging to God" it also means "a kingly majesty of the Messiah." It refers to the supremacy of Christ in all things, as the ruler king from whom all blessings flow. Think for just a moment about the incredible reality that as we worship the King we are being changed by His glory. This verse shows us that there are levels of the glory and that the longer we spend in the presence of Jesus, the deeper we are immersed in deeper levels of His presence. It also says that as we continually behold His glory, we are being continually changed as we grow in maturity in Christ. God can miraculously change us in just a moment when we encounter His glory, but in order for us to grow in maturity in Christ, we must choose to keep coming back to behold the source of the glory. As we behold Jesus, we are continually being transformed to look more and more like Him. As we go out, we reflect that same glory. The glory shining in the life of a believer has the power to illuminate the darkness around us. It is impossible to hide when you have truly been transformed by His glory.

As we go out, we must recognize that our first call is not unto a mission but unto Jesus Himself. Our first call is to gaze upon His glory and worship Him in Spirit and in truth; to be transformed by His word and refined by the fire of the Holy Spirit until everything about us shines brightly with His glory. This is the call of the Lord for each of us: to hear and answer His call to follow Him wherever He may lead. Then we can be transformed by His Holy fire, empowered, refined and sanctified by His blood until we reflect His glory in everything we do. We are then sent out, as carriers of His love, fire and glory to preach the gospel in a world bound by darkness. God is inviting you on the greatest adventure of your life. He is inviting you into the Fire.

This is the call. What will your answer be?

Truly, I say to you, unless you turn and become like children, you will never enter the kingdom of heaven. Whoever humbles himself like this child is the greatest in the kingdom of heaven. -Matthew 18:3-4

Preaching the gospel in a stadium crusade in Reynosa.

Tent revivals in Reynosa!

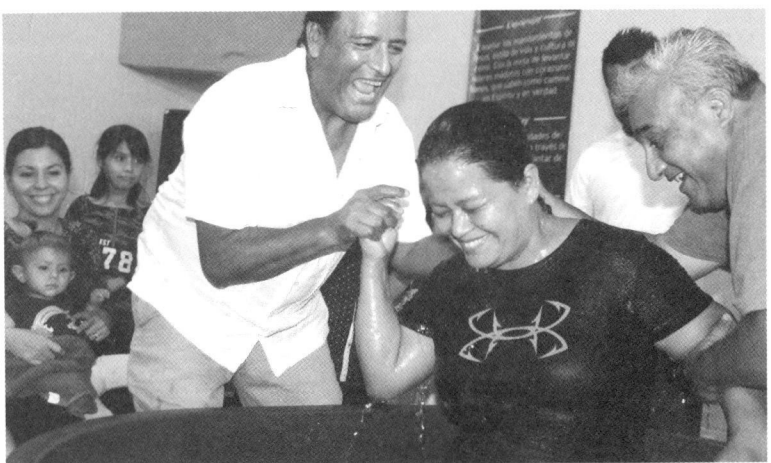

I have been crucified with Christ. It is no longer I who live, but Christ who lives in me. And the life I now live in the flesh I live by faith in the Son of God, who loved me and gave himself for me. -Galatians 2:20

About Kaleo International

Kaleo is a word taken from Biblical Greek that means "the call." Kaleo International is a missionary sending organization dedicated to training laborers to the harvest. We offer schools of missions and leadership every year.

The School of Missions is designed to equip missionaries through inner healing, theology, and practical outreach opportunities. The Leadership School is for leaders and pastors to gain knowledge in church planting and leadership.

Kaleo is dedicated to the vision of planting local churches with the DNA of revival. This international movement is a relational family that connects our local churches and missionaries around the world.

You can find out more about the work of Kaleo International on:

- 🌐 www.kaleointernational.org
- (f) Kaleo International
- (o) @kaleointernational

If you want to:

- Invite Joshua and/or Olivia to speak at your church, conference, or event.
- To plant a Kaleo Church.
- Become a missionary with us.

Please contact us to admin@kaleointernational.org or call/Whats App us at +52-899-334-2161.